Introduction

Today the 1930s are remembered for the period of the great Depression followed by the years of Appeasement, when the politicians of the European democracies vied with each other to accede to the demands of the dictators. However, for the P&O Company the early 1930s meant the introduction of the first 'White Sisters', the *Strathnaver* and *Strathaird*. They were a great boost to the company's fortunes and seemed like a breath of fresh air to the Merchant Marine. At over 22,000 gross tons they were the largest P&O vessels to take to the water up to that time, but the most striking change was the new livery. In place of P&O's traditional black hull, stone-coloured upperworks and black funnel, these latest ships were painted white all over with buff-coloured funnels. Critics of the colour scheme called it a gimmick and a novelty which would soon be replaced, but the travelling public loved it and it was an instant success.

Four years after the original 'White Sisters' came the *Strathmore*, followed two years later by the *Stratheden* and the ill-fated *Strathallan*. Each vessel was an improvement on its predecessor but, only 18 months after the last of the ships had entered service, war broke out again in Europe and the five 'White Sisters' left their peacetime routes and roles to become troop transports. At the end of the war there were only four left and they had been hard used during those dark years. Soon after the end of the Second World War the 'White Sisters' were eclipsed by two new vessels, *Himalaya* and *Chusan* which were constructed to replace lost tonnage and to modernize the fleet. The last of the *Straths* was sold by P&O in the mid-1960s, just as the age of the passenger liner was in decline, but they had represented the P&O Company in the heyday of sea travel and they are remembered with nostalgic affection by many people. This book is a tribute to those magnificent ships, P&O's five 'White Sisters'.

Neil McCart
Cheltenham
August 1994

To Caroline & Louise

Front Cover: The celebrated painting by Norman Wilkinson of the *Stratheden* at an Eastern port. (P&O)

Back Cover: A typical 1930s advertisement for cruises and voyages aboard the *Strathnaver* and the *Strathaird*. It is a style in use again by P&O Cruises in the 1990s. (P&O)

Inside Front Cover: The *Strathaird* undergoes her trials on the Clyde in January 1932. (P&O)

Inside Back Cover: The *Strathnaver* at Sydney after her post-war refit. (P&O)

Jacket Design: Caroline McCart
© Neil McCart/FAN PUBLICATIONS 1994
ISBN: 0 9519538 4 2

Typesetting By: Highlight Type Bureau Ltd, 31 Briggate, Shipley, West Yorkshire BD17 7EG

Printing By: The Amadeus Press Ltd, 517 Leeds Road, Huddersfield, West Yorkshire HD2 1YJ

Famous British Liners

P&O's Five White Sisters

The *Strath* Liners Of The 1930s

b

Contents

Chapter One – The First White Sisters 2

Chapter Two – New Standards Of Comfort 5

Chapter Three – Maiden Voyage.......................11

Chapter Four – A Royal Sponsor 19

Chapter Five – The Years Of Peace 26

Chapter Six – The Last White Sisters 30

Chapter Seven – The Uneasy Peace.....................41

Chapter Eight – War Comes To Europe..............47

Chapter Nine – Troopin' 53

Chapter Ten – Operation Torch 56

Chapter Eleven – Peace At Last........................66

Chapter Twelve – The Return To Trade..............69

Chapter Thirteen – The 1950s...........................75

Chapter Fourteen – The Final Years 87

Published By FAN PUBLICATIONS
17 Wymans Lane, Cheltenham, GL51 9QA, England. Fax & Tel 01242 580290

Chapter One

The First 'White Sisters'

When the First World War ended in November 1918 the P&O Company's mail service to Australia, a trade which had been built up over 65 years, had been all but abandoned. During the war the ships had been withdrawn from service to serve the nation either as armed merchant cruisers, troop transports or hospital ships. Before the war, between 1903 and 1914, the Australian service had been maintained largely by the 'M' class ships, ten of which had been built in the Edwardian years, all of them of about 10,000 gross tons. However, during the Great War six of these had been lost as a result of enemy action and for at least 12 months after the Armistice the other four vessels of the class were retained by the Admiralty as troopships. By 1920, three of the four ships, *Morea, Malwa* and *Mantua* were back on the Australian run together with the new, three-funnelled ships, *Naldera* and *Narkunda*. Although the latter two vessels were completed in 1918 and 1920 respectively, they were designed in 1913 and they were almost outdated when they entered service.

During the early 1920s four more vessels joined the mail route between London and Brisbane, these being the 16,000-tonners *Moldavia* and *Mongolia* and the larger 20,000-tonners *Mooltan* and *Maloja*. The first two ships were powered by steam turbines and the latter two by the trusted steam reciprocating engines which, although they had reliability, were slower than the former type. By the late 1920s the Edwardian 'M' class ships were well and truly outdated, having been built when class divisions in Britain were well defined, and their public rooms must have seemed quite out of fashion in the enlightened 1920s. The Great War, and particularly the conditions on the Western Front, had accelerated the breakdown in class divisions, and of course the war itself had brought about the emancipation of women in society. The old smoking rooms on the 'M' class ships, which were 'out of bounds' to women passengers and which had the atmosphere of the exclusive 'gentlemen's club', were behind the times. But the main factor which dated the vessels, the oldest of which was only 25 years of age, was their slow speed - less than 15 knots - and the fact that they carried twice as many first class passengers as second class.

The trend after the First World War, when emigration from Europe to the antipodes increased, was for more passengers to travel second class, whilst the demand for the first class accommodation decreased slightly. Many of the emigrants were skilled workers and tradesmen who wished to get away from the unemployment and the economic crises which marked those years. Australia in particular seemed to offer people most hope for the future and the demand for berths on both the mail steamers and the 'Branch Line' ships was high.

In those inter-war years the P&O service between London and India was as important as the route to Australia and, although all the ships which were *en route* to both the Far East and the antipodes called at Bombay and Colombo, there had always been a separate service to India. Some famous vessels had been built specifically for the route, including the *Rome* of 1881, the *Peninsular* of 1888, the *Caledonia* of 1894, the *Kaisar i Hind* and the brand new *Viceroy of India*.

By the end of the 1920s there was a need to replace the old 'M' class ships with new and larger vessels which could cater for the more sophisticated travelling public and keep pace with the latest ideas in ship construction and propulsion machinery. The vessels would have to steam at speeds which would render the company's separate Indian service unnecessary, and which would reduce the travelling time to Australia. The ships would have to be able to transit the Suez Canal and also be able to accommodate the Indian and Australian passengers. The new vessels would also have

The first of P&O's 'White Sisters', the *Strathnaver,* was launched from Vickers Armstrong's Barrow shipyard on 5 February 1931, by Lady Janet Bailey, a daughter of Lord Inchcape, the chairman of the P&O Company. This view shows the vessel as she thunders down the slipway.
(Vickers PLC)

18 July 1931, and the almost completed *Strathnaver* is moved into the centre of the dock to make way for the newly launched *Strathaird*. *(Sankey Collection)*

substantial cargo space, for in those days the mail steamers relied heavily on cargo revenues for profitability. Therefore, in the latter part of 1929, just before the 'Wall Street Crash' in New York, the veteran chairman of the P&O Company, the Rt Hon The Earl of Inchcape, set in motion negotiations which would lead to the launch of the first of the 'White Sisters'.

Although Vickers Armstrong of Barrow-in-Furness had never built any vessels for the P&O Company, between 1924 and 1928 they built a series of four very successful 20,000-tonners for the Orient Line. So when Lord Inchcape asked for tenders for two 22,000-ton ships, the Managing Director of the Barrow-based company, Commander C.W. Craven*, was determined to obtain the order, which would guarantee jobs for his work-force during lean times in the shipbuilding industry. Commander Craven, it is said, pursued Lord Inchcape relentlessly in an effort to secure the order and the industrialist, Sir Basil Zaharoff, was authorized to negotiate on behalf of Vickers. According to Lord Inchcape: 'The contract for these two steamers was arranged in Monte Carlo in December 1929, between Sir Basil Zaharoff and myself.' He went on to joke about the meeting thus: 'Had it not been that I was in rather a generous frame of mind owing to my having won 100 francs in the Casino, I think I might have squeezed a little more out of Sir Basil than I succeeded in doing, but there it is.' In fact the cost of the vessels to P&O was £2¹/₂ million, which at the time was a substantial order

for any shipyard.

In January 1930 the order for the two ships was officially placed and in April that year the first keel plates were laid for what were known as yard numbers 663 and 664, *Strathnaver* and *Strathaird* respectively. Just ten months later the first of the ships was ready for launching, and the ceremony took place on Thursday 5 February 1931. At just after midday Lady Janet Bailey, a daughter of Lord Inchcape and wife of Lt-Colonel F.G.G. Bailey RA, a director of the P&O Company, smashed a bottle of Australian wine on the bows of the *Strathnaver*, before sending her stern first down the slipway into the Walney Channel to the cheers of the dignitaries and work-force, who had assembled for the event. At a luncheon which followed, Sir Herbert A. Lawrence GCB, the chairman of Vickers Armstrong, thanked Lady Janet for making the journey to Barrow to launch the ship so gracefully and he presented her with a small gift to mark the occasion. In the absence of Lord Inchcape he asked her to convey the thanks of the people of Barrow to her father in providing the wages of his work-force. It was an indication of just how reliant the town was on the shipbuilding works. He remarked on the empty berths in his shipyard, which was one of those with more employment than most, and he congratulated Sir James Lithgow, the chairman of National Shipbuilders Security Ltd, on the progress he had made putting redundant shipyards out of commission. He regarded this as the industry improving its own position without

* Later Sir Charles W. Craven

government assistance, a theme which would not be out of place today.

The launch of yard number 664, *Strathaird*, followed on Saturday 18 July 1931, and this time Lord Inchcape attended the ceremony, having arrived in Barrow aboard his yacht *Rover*. Despite the fact that he was nearly 80 years old he was still a tremendously busy man, and for two days before the launch of the *Strathaird* he toured the *Strathnaver*, which was fitting out. The fact that the ceremony took place on a Saturday afternoon enabled thousands of local people to witness the event and excursion trips were made by both 'charabanc' and rail from Morecambe and the surrounding area to Barrow. Originally it had been intended that Lady Inchcape should perform the ceremony, but owing to ill health she had gone to Freiburg in Germany to consult a specialist. Her place was taken by her eldest daughter, Lady Margaret Shaw, the wife of the Hon Alexander Shaw, who would succeed Lord Inchcape as the next chairman of P&O. This time the luncheon preceded the event and there was a distinguished list of guests which included the High Commissioner for India and the chairman of Lloyd's. The ceremony passed off without a hitch and on a bright, sunny afternoon the *Strathaird* entered the water and was towed to her fitting-out berth alongside her sister, *Strathnaver*.

After the ceremony the guests went to the executive dining-room at the works where Sir Herbert Lawrence presided. After presenting Lady Shaw with a diamond brooch as a memento, which Lord Inchcape said, '...ought to go to her mother', Sir Herbert delivered his speech, the theme of which was again the shortage of orders and the unemployment which was looming for his work-force at Vickers Armstrong. Once the *Strathnaver* and *Strathaird* had been delivered there were no further merchant ships on the stocks and there had been no enquiries for many months, so it was clear that Vickers Armstrong faced a difficult period. Lord Inchcape had few words of comfort and although the *Strathnaver* and *Strathaird* were the two largest vessels built for the P&O Company, shipping was passing through troublesome times and it was not absolutely certain that their net earnings would be sufficient to pay the enormous sums of interest owed to the builders and earn a profit for the company. The only crumbs of comfort for the shipbuilders were Lord Inchcape's closing words: 'When times improve mayhap we may meet again at Barrow to launch another P&O steamer, always provided, of course, that your quotation is attractive, as I am sure it will be.' After the speech a telegram from Lady Inchcape was read to the guests, which perhaps sums up the reputation of the P&O Company : 'I hope the *Strathaird's* home for many years to come will be on the sea, navigated, handled and cared for by the capable, experienced and trustworthy commanders, officers and engineers of the P&O Company.'

The second of the three-funnelled 'White Sisters', the *Strathaird*, on the slipway at the Barrow shipyard shortly before her launch.   *(Sankey Collection)*

Chapter Two

New Standards Of Comfort

The design of the *Strathnaver* and *Strathaird* was the 'brainchild' of Lord Inchcape and was a complete contrast to all previous P&O vessels. Apart from the *Caledonia* in 1894 and the *Salsette* of 1908, the company ships had been painted in what can only be described as a drab livery of a black hull, stone-coloured superstructure and black funnels. It was true of course that in the days of coal-fired boilers these colours were far more practical, for when the bunkers were replenished it was a filthy business and the all-pervading coal dust found its way into every nook and cranny. Added to this were the copious quantities of soot deposits which resulted from the coal-fired boilers. However, in the late 1920s, when the far cleaner oil-fired boilers came into general use, it was clear that the white livery could be kept clean and psychologically, in the days before air-conditioning, it gave the feeling of coolness in tropical climes. Today of course the *Straths* are best remembered for their white hulls and superstructure, together with their buff funnels, which contributed to their great success with the public. At the time this new colour scheme had its critics and some people considered it a gimmick, but generally it was welcomed and set a precedent for all future mail ships right up to the *Canberra* of the 1960s.

The names of the new ships broke with the past too, when generally speaking names of eastern cities, towns and areas had been used, such as *Khedive, Peshawur, Coromondel, Mooltan* and *Maloja,* with a splendid ring about them in colonial times. *Strathnaver,* however, was taken from the first title of Lord Inchcape, the P&O chairman, and is itself the valley which runs from the Atlantic Ocean on the north coast of Scotland to Loch Naver. *Strathaird's* name was derived from the title of Sir William Mackinnon, the founder of the

British India Company, and is the name of a headland on the south of the Isle of Skye.

The first two 'White Sisters' had a distinctive appearance with their superstructure, in comparison with the older company vessels, seeming to tower up from the quayside which, together with the three large funnels, appealed immediately to the public. In fact the compact boilers in the two vessels only required one funnel, but in the late 1920s public opinion favoured more funnels as an indication of greater power. In the case of *Strathnaver* and *Strathaird* the first and third funnels were dummies and it was even said that, if viewed from the correct angle, daylight could be seen beneath their bases.

Another unusual feature of the two ships was the main propulsion machinery which, like the *Viceroy of India* of 1929, was the turbo-electric type. Indeed, it was the success of the *Viceroy* which led to its use in the first two *Straths*. Both ships were twin-screw vessels powered by two synchronous three-phase electric motors, built by the British Thompson-Houston Company. The power for these motors was supplied by two 750kW turbo-alternators, which in turn were driven by superheated steam which was provided at 425psi and 725°F by four oil-fired Yarrow water-tube boilers. The machinery developed 28,000 SHP and gave the ships a speed of 22 knots. This type of machinery has always been more widely used in US ships, particularly by the US Navy between the wars. One of the main advantages, from the passenger's point of view, was the quieter and smoother running of the ship with, it was claimed, far less vibration.

As has already been mentioned, the First World War broke down many of the entrenched class divisions within British society and although the two new liners, like their

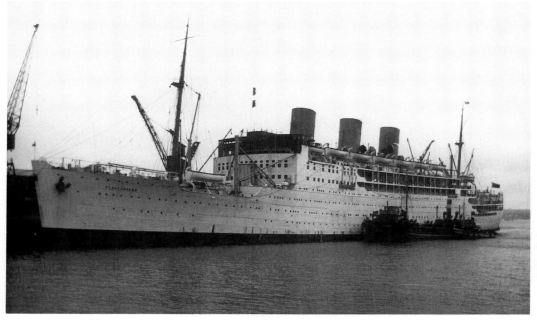

The first two 'White Sisters' had a distinctive appearance with their superstructure, in comparison with older company vessels, seeming to tower up from the quayside which, together with the three large funnels, appealed immediately to the public. This view shows the *Strathnaver* at Southampton.

(F.R. Sherlock)

The *Strathnaver's* first class Lounge was a finely proportioned room, the decoration of which was Italian in conception. This view shows the compartment looking forward.

(Author's Collection)

The *Strathnaver's* first class Reading and Writing Room was aft of the Lounge on the starboard side of the ship and was panelled in English cedar, with Queen Anne style furniture.

(Author's Collection)

The first class Smoking Room in the *Strathnaver* was *en suite* with the Reading and Writing Room and was decorated in a typically Scottish style. The chimney, which embodied a wrought-iron grate, was modelled on an original in Edinburgh's Holyrood Palace.

(Author's Collection)

The first class Reading and Writing Room in the *Strathaird*. Apart from the furnishings it was identical to that in her sister ship.

(Author's Collection)

The tourist class Verandah Café in the *Strathnaver*. It was situated on D Deck above the Lounge.

(Author's Collection)

predecessors, were to be two-class ships, what had been the second class became the 'tourist' class with much improved standards of accommodation and comfort. It proved a great success, for over the years the tourist class became popular with its reputation for less formality than the first class.

The layout of the passenger accommodation in both the *Strathnaver* and *Strathaird* was identical and although the decoration and furnishing varied in each, a detailed description of the former will suffice. The 488 first class passengers were accommodated on A, B, C, D, E and F Decks, with the single and two-berth cabins situated on the latter four decks. Also on D Deck there was one special Viceregal Suite, a cabin with a verandah sitting-room with picture windows, a bedroom and a bathroom suite. There were also 12 de luxe cabins, each with its own private bathroom, a facility which today's passengers take for granted. The Boat Deck, also called A Deck, was set aside exclusively as the first class games and sports area. The first class public rooms were on B Deck. Forward was the Lounge, and aft of it a Reading and Writing Room, which was panelled in English cedar, with Queen Anne furniture of walnut. The chairs and settees were covered in floral fabric and this, together with the natural light through decorated stained-glass windows, gave the room a charming and comfortable appearance. The Smoking Room, which was *en suite* with the Reading and Writing Room, was decorated in a typically Scottish style, giving it a handsome appearance. The panelling was of wire-brushed grey oak, and the chimney embodied a wrought-iron grate, which was modelled on an original in the Palace of Holyrood in Edinburgh. The scheme was completed by the addition of a painted panel depicting Bonnie Prince Charlie raising his standard at Glenfinnan on 19 August 1745, and by the introduction of various armorial devices in carved wood and stained glass. The furniture in this room was reproduction Jacobean style.

The most widely used room was of course the Lounge and the decoration of this finely proportioned saloon was Italian in conception. The walls were relieved by a dado in walnut, with a cream sycamore filling and a decorative coloured frieze, and blue lacquered Corinthian pillars and pilasters supported a handsome deeply corniced ceiling. There was a finely designed fireplace, set in an ample panelled recess, while wrought-iron door grilles added to the room's attraction. The diffused artificial lighting was of a novel character in the early 1930s and it was amplified by panelled lights grouped upon sconces of a classical design. The Verandah Café, which was aft on B Deck and which overlooked the swimming-pool, reproduced the style of a Spanish sun parlour with motifs from 'La Casa Greco'. Fine wrought-iron grilles to the windows and bar front contributed to the room's distinction and in the window bays tiled fountains added to the cool effect of the fine interior. The ceiling, which was gracefully trussed with carved beams, found a handsome response in the comfortable chairs and settees with which the room was furnished.

Just aft of the Verandah Café and beneath it on C Deck was the first class swimming-pool in its own deckhouse, the sides of which could be hinged up when weather permitted. Around the pool itself were large sliding windows and moving glass screens which could be opened up to admit fresh air. The adjacent swimmers' walk, which was paved with black and green marble, was one of the most popular resorts in the ship, second only to the pool itself. The first class dining saloon was on F Deck and the general effect of charming originality was achieved by a blend of English and French contemporary styles. Natural light and fresh air were admitted through large double windows fitted with glass louvres and decorative bronze grilles, while artificial light was derived from a series of shallow coffered fittings placed in the ceiling. The furniture was of bleached mahogany (in the *Strathaird* it was Macassar ebony and sycamore), with textile chair coverings copied from old needlework patterns. The panelling, in choice Sanara wood, completed the setting of this attractive room.

The *Strathnaver's* tourist class Lounge, which was panelled in natural mahogany with sycamore bands. The bookcases can be seen at the far end of the room.

(Author's Collection)

The 668 tourist class passengers were accommodated in two-and four-berth cabins on G and H Decks, with a Lounge and promenade space on E Deck and a Smoking Room and promenade aft on F Deck. In addition they had their own Games and Sports area on D Deck.

The handsome Lounge had gracefully panelled walls in natural mahogany, inlaid with sycamore bands, and large windows which gave the room an attractive air. The furniture was of golden sycamore, with comfortable settees, easy chairs and card-tables, and bookcases stacked with volumes for the use of passengers. The Smoking Room on F Deck was panelled in light grey oak with effective wall motifs in ebonised wood and was amply furnished with large settees and comfortable easy chairs, together with card-tables and writing-tables. The floor was covered with soft, warmly tinted rubber tiles. Quaint lanterns provided the lighting, while tall, square-paned windows opened on to the tourist Promenade Deck. The spacious tourist class dining saloon was also on F Deck and as an introduction to the new tourist class it offered high quality comfort and a unique character. The walls were handsomely panelled in light oak with contemporary features, and the room was furnished with comfortable armchairs and restaurant tables; here too the floor was of rubber tiling. Glass jalousie windows were fitted over the ports in order to give a decorative effect while still allowing maximum natural light to enter. Again, in keeping with the new tourist class, the cabins on both ships were

attractive, cool, white rooms, with plenty of space and every convenient fitting. Each had a wash-basin with running hot and cold water, together with a commodious wardrobe, chest of drawers and stowage space for small personal items of baggage. Today these facilities are essential in any hotel or ship, but in the early 1930s, hot and cold running water in particular, was a luxury in the tourist class. Although none of the tourist class cabins were fitted with private baths, there were plenty of bathrooms on each deck, which were supplied with salt water.

The accommodation for the ship's company would seem poor by today's standards, but in 1931 it was roomy and comfortable. The master and executive officers were berthed beneath the bridge on the Boat Deck and the engineers and electrical officers were accommodated on E Deck. The European and Goan crew members were quartered forward on E, F and G Decks. Lieutenant Commander John de Broughton RCN recalls his service in the *Strathnaver* when, as the senior of the three cadets on board, he occupied, with his two colleagues, a small cabin next to the Radio Office, which overlooked the starboard side of the Boat Deck. He comments that, 'Although our accommodation was extremely cramped, we were made fairly comfortable by the service of a Goan steward.'

Although it would be another 40 years before the class barriers were removed completely, the *Strathnaver* and *Strathaird* led the way in this social revolution.

The *Strathaird's* tourist class dining saloon on F Deck. As an introduction to the new tourist class it offered high quality comfort and a unique character.

(Author's Collection)

The *Strathaird's* first class sports deck. Compare this with the post-war view of the *Strathnaver* in Chapter Twelve.

(Author's Collection)

Chapter Three

Maiden Voyage

The first of the two 'White Sisters' to be completed was the *Strathnaver* and she was commanded by 57-year-old Captain Basil James Ohlson DSO RD RNR. He had been at sea since 1892 and in the early 1930s was one of a dwindling number of seamen who had started their careers under sail. His first ship was the *Derwent*, a full-rigged clipper of 1,970 tons which in its day contended with the famous clippers of the time, including the *Cutty Sark*. He then joined the *Rodney*, a 1,500-ton clipper, which also carried 60 passengers in comparative luxury for those days. He joined the P&O in 1896 as Fifth Officer of the *Parramatta* and subsequently commanded such well known vessels as the *Moldavia, Macedonia, Mongolia* and the *Viceroy of India*. He had been particularly enthusiastic about the *Viceroy of India* and considered her to be the best steering ship in which he had ever sailed. There had been no need to use her engines when rounding the bends of the Suez Canal and, according to his son, he always described her manoeuvring capabilities thus: 'She was as quick and easy to handle as a steam pinnace.'

The *Strathnaver* left Barrow on Wednesday 26 August 1931 and it was reported in the Press at the time that, 'She looked a fine sight, with her white hull and three yellow funnels as she steamed down the Walney Channel to the open sea.' After dry docking in the Gladstone Dock in Liverpool she steamed north to the Clyde where she underwent her trials, before being handed over to the P&O Company on Wednesday 2 September, a week after she had left Barrow.

The trials had been a success and she attained speeds of over 22 knots, although on her Australian voyages and whilst cruising, she would require only 16 to 18 knots with two boilers and one turbo-generator in action. On the evening that she completed her trials she anchored off Greenock and embarked a number of guests for the voyage round to Tilbury. These included Lord and Lady Inchcape, the High Commissioners for Australia and India and officials of both the P&O Company and Vickers Armstrong. After dinner the next day, as the *Strathnaver* neared Tilbury, Lord Inchcape made a speech in which he expressed confidence that the ship would do credit to her builders and owners. He referred to the terrible slump in world trade and how it had hit the shipping industry and he praised Mr Ramsay MacDonald and Mr Philip Snowden for forming a national government, which he was sure would, '...save the British Empire'. His speech mirrored the nation's anxieties and hopes in those depressed years.

The *Strathnaver* left Tilbury on 1 October 1931 for Brisbane and seven days later she arrived in Marseilles, where she was joined by many passengers who had travelled by rail on the special Calais to Marseilles 'Bombay Express', as it was known. The train had left Calais on the previous day and it enabled the passengers to save at least four days on the journey and in addition, mail was embarked which had been posted four days after the ship had sailed from London.

After making the transit of the Suez Canal on 14/15 October, Captain Ohlson berthed his new command

The *Strathnaver's* first master was Captain Basil James Ohlson DSO RD RNR, who had been at sea since 1892, and in the early 1930s he was one of a dwindling number of seamen who had started their careers under sail. Here he is seen with his deck officers by the *Strathnaver's* forward funnel.

(B.A. Ohlson)

A magnificent view of the *Strathnaver*, taken on 1 September 1931, as she underwent her trials on the Clyde.

After dry docking in the Gladstone Dock in Liverpool, the *Strathnaver* steamed north to the Clyde where she underwent her trials before being handed over to the P&O Company on Wednesday 2 September 1931.

(Author's Collection)

alongside Circular Quay in Sydney Harbour on the morning of Thursday 12 November 1931, and she was the largest vessel and the first turbo-electric ship to visit the port. By this time one awkward feature of her propulsion machinery had become evident and one of the Sydney pilots told Captain Ohlson's son about the ship's arrival in these words: 'One incident will be of interest. He brought *Strathnaver* to Sydney on her maiden voyage and she was the first electro-turbine ship with inturning propellers to reach those shores, and a lack of manoeuvrability in confined waters had manifested itself more than once during the voyage. In addition to going aground in the Suez Canal outward bound, she proved difficult to berth at other Australian ports before reaching Sydney so our pilots were ready to cope with her clumsiness. The senior pilot at the time, the late Captain Hill, recalled how he went aboard at the Heads and congratulated Captain Ohlson on his fine new command, with a rider that he understood *Strathnaver* might be difficult to berth that morning. Captain Ohlson retorted, "Well Captain, you will find this out for yourself before we get alongside." As they approached the berth the pilot pulled the bridge telegraph - "port engine half astern", and Captain Ohlson looked amazed and remarked, "You'll never get my ship alongside with such a direction." However, just at the psychological moment, a gust of wind caught them broadside on and the ship slid alongside like a ferry boat. Captain Ohlson's final words were, "My apologies pilot, you can obviously handle my ship better than I can." Modest words from a captain who served his time in the four-masted China clippers and was noted throughout the company for his seamanship.'

Strathnaver had followed the traditional P&O route via Marseilles, Suez, Aden, Bombay, Colombo, Fremantle, Adelaide, Sydney and Brisbane. She had been fully booked in both classes, as it was the busy season for passengers to Australia and there had been a great demand for berths aboard her. She arrived back at Tilbury in January 1932, just before her sister ship the *Strathaird* arrived in the port from the Clyde.

The *Strathaird* had left Barrow on 6 January 1932 for dry docking in Liverpool and before she left the port Mr Alexander Shaw, P&O's deputy chairman and a director of the Bank of England, entertained a large number of guests to lunch on board where he made a major international speech wearing 'both his hats'. It was no surprise to hear him tell his audience that, for the time being, the *Strathaird* represented the end of the post-1919 building effort by P&O. He also told them that during the world-wide Depression the company was doing its best to keep the Red Ensign flying on the seven seas, but it was clear that the weekly service to India could not be guaranteed. The Depression had indeed bitten deep and hard. Mr Shaw then turned his speech to the subject of war debts, an issue which still held the attention of economists and world statesmen. The speech was widely reported in the world's Press and so it gave the new ship plenty of publicity.

On the evening of Saturday 9 January the *Strathaird* left the Mersey and steamed north for the Clyde where she carried out her trials before being handed over to the company and leaving for Tilbury. From there she left on her maiden voyage to Brisbane on Friday 12 February 1932. She was commanded by Captain W.P. Townshend RD RNR, who had joined the P&O Company in 1896 as had Captain Ohlson of the *Strathnaver*. She had on board 700 passengers, amongst whom were Dame Clara Butt the famous singer, and several other titled people. Although more passengers were joining the ship at Marseilles, she was not fully booked for the outward voyage, which at that time of the year was not unusual for the main stream of passengers was homeward bound. Mr R.C. Temple, who was an Assistant Purser on the voyage recalls: 'The lofty superstructure towering up from the quayside in Tilbury made the older P&O ships look very low in comparison. The voyage was fairly normal, but I do remember tensions between the senior officers who, no doubt, found these innovative ships at first difficult in control and management compared with the old ships. *Strathnaver* had gone before us and had stolen our thunder, but we were mobbed by thousands of Australians coming aboard to view the ship at each Australian port.'

The maiden voyages of both the 'White Sisters' were an unqualified success, but the world depression in trade continued to worry the P&O management. At a dinner for the Lord Mayor of London held on board the *Strathnaver* at Tilbury in May 1932, Mr Alexander Shaw, who was the company's acting chairman in the absence of Lord Inchcape who was seriously ill, appealed to Britons to travel in British ships. Ten days later, on 23 May, Lord Inchcape died on board his yacht *Rover* at Monaco and Mr Shaw took over as

The *Strathnaver* at Tilbury during September 1931, prior to her maiden voyage to Brisbane. The cliff-like appearance of her superstructure can be seen clearly in this bow view.

(Vickers PLC)

chairman. Lord Inchcape had been at the helm since that fateful month of August 1914 and his last contribution to the company's fleet had been the two 'White Sisters'. He had lived to see both ships embarked upon their careers, and the building programme was to be continued by his successor, but not until the economic situation improved.

In July 1932 the *Strathaird* made the first of her UK cruises. She sailed from Tilbury for a 14-day cruise to the Mediterranean with 600 first class passengers on board. Mr G.S. Stone of Lutterworth, who was on the P&O staff, travelled on a similar cruise in the *Strathaird* with his wife in September that year, when for the first time the company were giving their employees a concessionary rate. Mr & Mrs Stone occupied a four-berth cabin on G Deck, with the top two bunks folded back, for £14. The whole ship was open to all the passengers, with those accommodated aft using the tourist class dining-saloon. Mr Stone recalls: 'There were very few cabins with bathrooms, the baths being situated along each alleyway, with a Goan steward in attendance who would fill the bath. It was seawater, with a little fresh water for after use. There was a Race Night, Fancy Dress Ball and a Gala Night, which were all great fun and we had a gentleman on board who was a bookmaker; on Race Night he managed to swindle the tote which was run by the Assistant Pursers. The sequel to this was he and his wife were requested to take their meals in the after saloon.' Amongst the ports of call were Monte Carlo, Algiers and Vigo, very similar to today's cruise itineraries. Mr R.C. Temple also recalls the same cruise

and the romantic sight of the floodlit *Strathaird* anchored off Monaco on a calm Mediterranean night.

By the spring of 1934 both ships were well established and extremely popular with travellers both on voyages and cruises. In May that year Captain Ohlson of the *Strathnaver* retired from the sea to take up an appointment as the P&O Agent in Malta. Two months later the *Strathaird* called in at Malta's Grand Harbour as part of a two-week Mediterranean cruise from Southampton, having called at Barcelona and Naples. During her stay in the port she embarked four extra passengers for the voyage home, the Misses Patricia and Pamela Mountbatten and their governess and nurse. Lord Mountbatten, their father, was at the time captain of a destroyer in Malta. The final port of call on the homeward leg of the cruise was Gibraltar, where the ship spent nine hours on 24 July. In those days passengers could take a shore excursion by horse and carriage to Main Street, Alameda Gardens and Rosia, up the Rock and return via the Eastern Beach, all for 6s-6d (32^1/2p). Today a tour for cruise passengers along a similar route costs nearly £20. But of course they were more leisurely times, and today it would be difficult to drive a horse and carriage around the overcrowded town. After leaving Gibraltar at 5pm that day, she arrived back in Southampton during the afternoon of Friday 27 July 1934.

The first two years' service for both ships had proved to be an unqualified success and it was clear that their critics had been proved wrong. Now, with economic conditions improving, P&O were about to launch a third 'White Sister'.

The *Strathaird* left Barrow in early January 1932 for docking in Liverpool and her trials on the Clyde. *(VSEL)*

On the route to Australia, via Suez, the first 'White Sisters', like the P&O steamers before them, regularly called at Port Sudan in the Red Sea. This unusual photograph, taken at that port, shows a group of passengers and local boys with either the *Strathnaver* or the *Strathaird* in the background.

(Southampton City Museums)

(*Vickers PLC*)

The *Strathaird* lies at 31 berth in Tilbury Docks, with the *Strathnaver* directly astern of her.

The *Strathnaver* arrives at Southampton Docks early one morning in the 1930s.

The *Strathnaver* in the Thames alongside the Tilbury Landing Stage.

(Alex Duncan)

During the 1930s cruising was a popular holiday for very wealthy people, but with the advent of the *Straths* P&O wanted to widen its appeal. This photograph shows one of the contemporary advertising posters for cruising in the first two 'White Sisters'.
(P&O)

Chapter Four

A Royal Sponsor

By the summer of 1934 the directors of P&O had been able to assess the performance and economics of the first two 'White Sisters', and as they were suitably impressed, they planned to build another, bigger ship and to improve even further their service between England, India and Australia. Together the P&O and Vickers' naval architects produced a particularly pleasing design, with a midships superstructure which was not as 'cliff-like' as the first two ships, and with only one funnel instead of three, which gave the new ship a graceful appearance. At nearly 24,000 gross tons and with an overall length of 640ft, she was the largest ship to be built for P&O at that time and it was a valuable order for Vickers Armstrong.

The new vessel was launched on Thursday 4 April 1935 and it was a major event at Barrow-in-Furness which was so heavily dependent on the shipbuilding industry. The ship's sponsor was the Duchess of York, who is today of course HRH the Queen Mother. Together with the Duke of York she arrived at Barrow's Furness Abbey Station by special train at 7.25pm on the day before the ceremony and the royal couple were driven away to Abbey House as the guests of Sir Charles and Lady Craven. At 10.30am the following day the royal guests left their hosts' house and went straight to the shipyard where, after inspecting guards of honour, they proceeded to the launching platform. The ceremony had been fixed for 11am, but as the high tide in the Walney Channel had already passed, at 10.53am the Duchess pulled the lever which released the launching triggers, saying, 'I name this ship the *Strathmore*. May God bless all those who sail in her.' As the

great white hull went stern first into the water, the sky cleared and there was a burst of brilliant sunshine, which appeared to be a good omen for the new ship. The name *Strathmore* was appropriate because not only was it in line with the first two 'White Sisters', but it was the family name of the Duchess's father, and his home, Glamis Castle, was situated in the valley of Strathmore, north of Dundee.

As the royal visitors toured the shipyard, the tugs were towing the new ship to the Buccleuch Dock to lie alongside the Orient Line's *Orion* which was already being fitted out, having been launched in December 1934. After being shown round the yard, which included a visit to the cruiser *Ajax,* the Duke and Duchess were driven to the Vickers Armstrong main offices for lunch. Also present at the gathering were the P&O chairman, Mr Alexander Shaw and Sir Charles Craven. Their speeches were far more optimistic than those which had been made four years earlier, now that the order books were fuller than they had been for some years. Parts of Alexander Shaw's speech would not have sounded out of place today as he reminded his audience that, 'The vessel which the Duchess of York has launched today is not only a new link of Empire. It is more. It is a link forged by British private enterprise without public assistance. His Royal Highness, as a sailor, knows that it means everything to this country that our merchant fleet should not be allowed to succumb in the grim struggle which it continues to wage against highly subsidized foreign competition.' He went on to announce that the Duchess of York had been good enough to allow her portrait to be painted by Mr Simon Elwes and to approve of a copy

The launch of the *Strathmore*, the third of the 'White Sisters', took place on Thursday 4 April 1935 and it was a major event at Barrow-in-Furness. The ship's sponsor was the Duchess of York, who is now the Queen Mother.

(P&O)

P. & O. 'STRATHMORE' - 1st CLASS SPORTS DECK

The *Strathmore's* first class Sports Deck looking aft. With only one funnel the deck was less cluttered than those on the earlier 'White Sisters'.

(Author's Collection)

The *Strathmore's* first class Reading and Writing Room, at the forward end of B Deck, was panelled in figured ash and French walnut. The portrait of HRH the Duchess of York can be seen over the fireplace at the left hand side of the photograph.

(Author's Collection)

Walking aft through the *Strathmore's* main foyer and past the two lifts there were entrances on both port and starboard sides to the Lounge, where the general theme of the décor was the rich blue of the carpets and floor coverings.

(Author's Collection)

The *Strathmore's* first class Verandah Café, which was aft of the dance space on B Deck.   *(Author's Collection)*

The *Strathmore's* first class dining saloon was on F Deck amidships and it was a well-designed room which could seat 258 passengers at one sitting.
(Author's Collection)

The *Strathmore* had accommodation for 665 tourist class passengers and special attention was given to their comfort. The tourist class Lounge was on E Deck and it was a wide, spacious area panelled in weathered sycamore and walnut.

(Author's Collection)

being made which would hang in the *Strathmore*. The original was presented to Her Royal Highness as a token of gratitude for her consenting to launch the ship.

The Duke of York, who would soon become King George VI, referred in his speech to the improvement in the shipbuilding industry and he congratulated, '...all those who have been associated with the design and building of the *Strathmore,* and I trust that she will always be a happy ship for all those who sail in her, and prove herself a worthy member of the fleet which is owned by the P&O.'

The *Strathmore* was about 8ft shorter than the first two sisters, but her beam, at 82ft, was slightly greater and at 23,428 gross tons she exceeded their tonnage by nearly 150 grt. The company chose steam turbines to drive the twin propellers directly through single-reduction gearing. Each propeller was powered by one high-pressure, one intermediate-pressure and one low-pressure turbine. The astern turbines consisted of one HP and one LP turbine in series. All the turbines were designed to run at 1,175 rpm and the gear ratio was such that, at this turbine speed, the propellers ran at 112 rpm. The steam generating installation in the boiler-rooms consisted of six oil-fired Babcock & Wilcox high-pressure superheat boilers, with a working pressure of 440 psi and a temperature of 750°F. Altogether the main propulsion machinery gave the ship a shaft horsepower of 24,000 and a speed of nearly 22 knots.

The *Strathmore* had accommodation on six decks for 445 first class passengers, 199 of whom would be in single-berth cabins while the remainder were in two-berth rooms. There were two de luxe cabins on D Deck, each comprising a sitting-room with verandah, a bedroom and a bathroom. On the same deck were eight more cabins with private bathrooms, and there were bathroom cabins on C Deck. The Boat Deck, or A Deck, was the first class games deck with an area of 275ft by 82ft, and not only was there provision for deck tennis and quoits, but it was also equipped with a full-size tennis court surrounded by nets. As with the first two *Straths,* the *Strathmore's* first class public rooms were on B Deck, with a Library and Writing Room at the forward end. It was panelled in figured ash and French walnut and the unusual shape forward was determined by the curve of the bridge front. Large bow windows were fitted at both sides which looked out on to an enclosed promenade. The ceiling rose inwards from the windows in a series of covings and over the fireplace was the portrait of the Duchess of York by Simon Elwes. Flanking the portrait, two finely figured walnut panels formed doors to bookcases which, together with two glazed cases at the outboard forward corners, contained the large library. Bronze-cased pillars lent an air of dignity to the room, while the bleached mahogany and pine furniture with rich green covers and toning curtains gave a feeling of luxury.

Continuing aft through the main foyer and past the two lifts there were entrances on both port and starboard sides to the Lounge, where the general tone of the décor was a rich blue for the carpets and floor coverings, relieved with silver and grey. The panelling was in cool brown and gold, and

The tourist class Smoking Room in the *Strathmore* was on F Deck and it was panelled in English oak.

(Author's Collection)

there was a silvered ceiling to the central couch roof. At the forward end there was a wide, full-height fitted mirror, which added to the spacious vista.

In the dance space aft of the Lounge, the casings and ceilings were painted in a soft ivory shade and coloured lighting effects were obtained from a raised dome and from several illuminated pillars. Both sides of the dance space were enclosed with full-height hinged, glazed screens which enabled dancing to take place in all weathers. However, the main reason for fitting these screens was to cut the cost of the Suez Canal dues which were calculated on the vessel's gross tonnage, reckoned in its turn on a ship's total volume of 'enclosed space'. Going aft again, one passed from the dancing space into the Verandah Café, which was a large room decorated simply but effectively.

On C Deck, just forward of the swimming-pool was an open-air Verandah Café. It was situated in a sheltered recess and simply decorated with painted and moulded horizontal bands. The first class children's nursery was also on C Deck and placed well forward of the bridge. Access to it was from the accommodation below, and port and starboard side doors opened on to large play decks. The nursery was panelled in silky oak with bandings in rosewood and carved inset panels of decorative lime showing contemporary transport. The furniture was covered in brightly patterned materials and there were plenty of toys to amuse the younger travellers, as well as their own paddling pool on the starboard side, just outside the playground.

The first class dining saloon, which was on F Deck amidships, could seat 258 passengers in one sitting. It was a well-designed room and its central feature was a large needlework tapestry panel depicting Glamis Castle situated in the wooded Plain of Strathmore, with the hazy outlines of the Grampian Mountains in the background. The panelling was in bleached cherry with a beautiful soft, warm tone, with bandings of cool brown-coloured walnut. The glazed entrance doors and screens, and the screens to the sidelights, were in aluminium with a matt silver finish. Just forward of the main saloon on the port side was a children's dining-room, which was panelled in Dutch elm with banding in Zebrano and certain features were picked out in bright colours. Seating was arranged for 36 youngsters in small armchairs, and with its bright decoration the room had a cheerful appearance which quite suited its purpose.

It was apparent that special attention had been given to the tourist class section for, as with the earlier sisters, the majority of the *Strathmore's* passengers, 665 in fact, would be accommodated in this part of the ship, in 280 two-, four- or six-berth cabins on F, G and H Decks. The dining saloon was on F Deck aft of the galley and pantries, and it could seat 332 passengers in one sitting. The room was panelled in matching oak and walnut, and windows gave diners a clear view aft. On the inboard side, glazed partitions screened the entrance hall, which gave access to the accommodation on the decks both above and below. Aft of the entrance hall and also on F Deck was the tourist Smoking Room, which was panelled in English brown oak veneer, with a decorative effect obtained by the introduction of broad oak bands of horizontal flat mouldings. A wide radiator surround in stone was fitted at the after end with a panel above it in finely figured and quartered burr oak. The forward end was relieved with a contemporary oil painting of a scene from *Strathmore,* set over an open staircase leading down to G Deck. The comfortable furniture, which was covered in red and fawn hide, was grouped conveniently throughout the room. The tourist class Lounge was on E Deck, above the Smoking Room, and it was a wide and spacious area panelled in weathered sycamore and walnut. The lovely colour of this veneer was further enhanced by shades of old rose and coral which were used in the fabric of the curtains and the furniture upholstery. Also on E Deck but forward and aft of the Lounge respectively, were the tourist swimming-pool and children's nursery. The latter room was particularly attractive, decorated as it was with oak panels of carved motifs inset on a background of jade green. There was direct access from the nursery to the deck and to the cabin accommodation below. The tourist class dancing space and Verandah Café were both situated on D Deck and the former, like its first class counterpart, was enclosed at the sides by hinged glass screens, which allowed the hall to be closed against cold, wet weather, or opened to the fresh air on hot days. In the Verandah Café

the designers concentrated on obtaining a bright and airy effect. The panelling was in light sycamore with decorated sections of ivory white spaced at intervals along the walls. Mirrors were freely used and at the forward end there was a wide stretch of double-glazed doors, while large windows looked out on to the tourist dancing space. In the words of a contemporary journal: 'It is not too much to say that the tourist passengers find a comfort and convenience, a catering to all their needs and wishes, and a beauty of decoration which no more than ten years ago would have been considered the last word in refinements in the first class accommodation.'

By late August 1935 work on the *Strathmore* was almost complete and on Wednesday 11 September that year she left Barrow for Liverpool to be dry docked. Just two days later on the evening of 13 September she steamed back down the Mersey and turned north for the Clyde and two days of acceptance trials. Despite windy conditions and severe squalls of rain, the results of her speed trials over the Arran measured mile were entirely satisfactory and the contract speed of 20 knots was exceeded, with a highest speed of 22.27 knots being attained. And so, on the afternoon of Sunday 15 September 1935, with the Firth of Clyde shrouded in a cold, grey, damp mist, the P&O house-flag was hoisted to the mast-head of the *Strathmore,* the newest of the 'White Sisters'.

This excellent view of the *Strathmore,* berthed in London's Tilbury Docks, shows her to have a more graceful appearance than the earlier 'White Sisters'. In 1935 she was the largest ship to be built for P&O.

(E.H. Cole)

Chapter Five

The Years Of Peace

On the evening of 15 September 1935, with her trials completed and now handed over to the P&O Company, the *Strathmore* embarked a number of passengers, including the Chancellor of the Exchequer, Sir John Simon, and Sir John Reith of the BBC, for the voyage to Tilbury. Despite gale force winds and heavy seas she managed to keep up a speed of 20 knots, but she was almost 12 hours late when she arrived in Tilbury on 17 September. Ten days later on 27 September she left for a 16-day shakedown cruise commanded by Captain W.T. Sudell, who had joined the P&O in the late 19th century and had had a distinguished career with the company. The cruise itinerary included Madeira, Dakar, the Canary Isles, and Cadiz, and the entire ship was first class on this occasion with fares starting at 30 guineas.

The *Strathmore's* maiden voyage was a special sailing to Bombay and she left Tilbury on the afternoon of Saturday 26 October 1935. Despite company efforts to play down the event, there was a great amount of speculation in the Press as to whether the ship would beat the *Viceroy of India's* speed record to Bombay. In fact there were two separate records, the first between London and Bombay and the second between Marseilles and Bombay. The *Viceroy's* time for the former, made in October 1934, was 15 days, 22 hours and 51 minutes, and for the latter, achieved a year earlier in October 1933, it was ten days, 23 hours and 14 minutes. As the *Strathmore* passed Gibraltar at 6pm on Tuesday 29 October everything seemed to augur well for a new speed record, although P&O took the trouble to announce that the new ship was not making any special efforts to break any records. Perhaps they were just making allowances for the vagaries of the north-east monsoon, which the *Strathmore* had still to encounter between Aden and her destination. In the event she tied up alongside Bombay's Ballard Pier at noon on Sunday 10 November 1935, which meant she had cut a day off the *Viceroy's* London-Bombay record and she had taken exactly ten days for the voyage from Marseilles. She had steamed at an average speed of 20.07 knots and the first class passengers sent a telegram to P&O's head office congratulating the comany on, '...the most successful voyage east of the *Strathmore* under Captain Sudell.' The third of the *Straths* was off to a spectacular start and she was obviously going to be as popular as the earlier two ships.

On her return to London the *Strathmore* made two winter cruises, the first on 21 December 1935 for 20 days to Madeira, the Canary Isles, Casablanca and Cadiz. The second lasted 30 days, calling at Madeira then crossing the Atlantic Ocean for stops at Kingston, Jamaica, Trinidad in Cuba and Bridgetown, Barbados. On the homeward leg she called at Las Palmas and Casablanca before arriving back in the UK on 10 February 1936. Her second voyage east was again to Bombay and it was Captain Sudell's final command before his retirement. The voyage got off to a bad start when, after leaving Tilbury on 15 February 1936, she was held up in the Thames by dense fog for 24 hours. Then, when she was off the west coast of Portugal she suffered mechanical problems to her starboard reduction gearing and she limped into Gibraltar on 20 February, five days after leaving Tilbury. There then followed a further three days' delay whilst her engineers, assisted by staff from the Royal Naval Dockyard, repaired the fault. She finally left Gibraltar on 23 February and from then on the voyage went smoothly and she was able to make up one of the four lost days. She finally arrived back in Tilbury at noon on 25 March and Captain R. Harrison DSO RD RNR took command. He had first gone to sea in Devitt & Moore's iron-built clipper *Hesperus* in 1895, and had joined P&O in 1899. Captain Harrison had been, for a time, ADC to King George V, an honour accorded to only four Merchant Navy officers and he was one of two P&O officers to walk in the King's funeral procession.

His first voyage in the *Strathmore* was somewhat special as one very distinguished passenger was Lord Linlithgow, who was on his way to take up his appointment as the Viceroy of India. When the ship stopped in Aden on 11 April 1936, the Viceroy designate gave a breakfast party on board at which Vice Admiral F.F. Rose, the naval C-in-C East Indies Station and the British Resident in Aden, attended. When the *Strathmore* sailed she was escorted from the harbour by destroyers and RAF aircraft from the new airfield in the colony at Khormaksar. It might be supposed today, with memories of Empire rapidly fading, that a passage with a new Viceroy of India to take up his duties, then returning with the retiring Viceroy on board, was a normal procedure. However, it had long been a tradition in British India that the old and the new viceroys did not meet on Indian soil and so by embarking the outgoing viceroy for the homeward voyage, the *Strathmore* was setting a different kind of record. One item of interest to today's reader is that the ship gained the highest praise from her distinguished passengers on both the outward and homeward voyages. Lord and Lady Willingdon, the retiring viceroy and vicereine, '...expressed themselves in terms of the highest praise of the comfort and stability of the ship. It was an excellent passage all the way, and although Lord Willingdon had unfortunately caught a chill which laid him up for a few days, he and Lady Willingdon had been most comfortable in their Viceregal Suite.' The couple had proved most popular with the first class passengers and it was noted that they mixed freely with the other passengers in the public rooms and on the Promenade Deck. Some passengers who had travelled on the 'Overland Express' from Marseilles went to Tilbury to meet the ship.

Mr R.C. Temple, an Assistant Purser, recalls Lord and Lady Willingdon as passengers between Marseilles and Bombay in the *Strathaird* during the early 1930s and he remembers that Lady Willingdon insisted on having purple-coloured deck quoits for herself (her favourite colour), and that the couple insisted that the Promenade Deck above their cabin be roped off and placed out of bounds to other passengers. Unfortunately for them a group of mischievous 'Aussies' decided to do early morning PT exercises on the forbidden area. He also recalls how Lady Willingdon took

The *Strathmore's* maiden voyage, which started from Tilbury on Saturday 26 October 1935, was a special sailing to Bombay. This excellent pre-war view shows the vessel at Tilbury's new Passenger Landing Stage. *(P&O)*

Captain Sudell and the officers of the *Strathmore*. *(P&O)*

It was 1936 before the *Strathmore* made her first visit to Australia and in this view she makes a fine sight as she steams through Sydney's picturesque harbour. *(P&O)*

over the Purser's Pekinese dog as a pet for the voyage and carried it ashore under her arm at the ceremonial landing in Bombay. Happily she did return the animal to its rightful owner before the ship sailed.

Both the *Strathnaver* and the *Strathmore* made a number of UK cruises during the summer of 1936. Mrs Olive Evans, who was a young lady of 26 at that time, remembers a 14-day cruise she made in the former ship. She shared a two-berth cabin in the after part of the ship which cost her £30. The vessel left Tilbury on 29 August 1936, bound for Madeira, Casablanca, Gibraltar, Lisbon, Bordeaux and Southampton. Mrs Evans recalls that the ship took four days to reach Madeira, where it anchored in Funchal Bay. During a sightseeing trip on the island she felt ill and later went to the ship's surgeon, who diagnosed mumps. She spent the remainder of the cruise in the isolation ward, which was at the after end of D Deck. She recalls the long days spent sitting in the shade on the small covered Promenade Deck, her only companion being the nurse who, when she was off duty, would sit with her. The ward itself, she recalls, was all white and airy and very pleasant with two beds in it, and a steward who brought meals. In those days such illnesses were taken very seriously and she remembers that when the ship did return to Southampton she was not allowed to go ashore until all the other passengers had disembarked, and even then a special gangway was put in place solely for her, in order that she did not come into contact with anyone else.

That summer the *Strathaird* was cruising in the Mediterranean, when she was on the central line of a total eclipse of the sun. She was off Hydra Island at the entrance to the Gulf of Athens, between Corfu and Athens at the time, and at 5am on the day of the eclipse her upper decks were packed with passengers to witness the event.

In 1937, Mr E.J. Read of Ringwood wrote to a number of shipping companies, enquiring about employment on board the ocean liners. After turning down a steward's position with Cunard he undertook and passed a trade test for a Third Cook's position on the *Strathnaver* and sailed with the ship for Bombay. He recalls his first arrival at Ballard Pier as an experience never to be forgotten. He remembers, '...the striking uniforms of the Maharaja's troops, Indian police in blue uniforms with a yellow head-dress, women in beautiful saris of exquisite colours, and as the passengers stepped ashore garlands of flowers were placed around their necks.' He also remembers some amusing moments during the voyage: 'Once in the Red Sea a boxing match was arranged by the crew, to amuse the passengers. A canvas awning, somewhat dotted with holes burnt by soot from the funnel, was placed over the ring. The captain and all the VIP guests were seated to one side and the boxers decided to have a "fun bout" with large "custard pies". When one opponent stepped aside a very large, messy custard pie landed well and truly in the midst of the captain's guests, much to the amusement of all present.' Mr Read also remembers the arrival at Fremantle on the outward voyage. It was the first landfall in Australia and all the crew members, nearly 500 in all, had to assemble on deck at 6am and hold out their hands for inspection by the port's health officers. A strange ritual, the reason for which he never found out.

In the autumn of 1936, with the three *Strath* liners all successfully in service and extremely popular with the travelling public, the directors of P&O placed two more orders with Vickers Armstrong. They were to be the last two *Strath* liners and they would join the older sisters for just 18 months, steaming the route to Australia and carrying holiday-makers from London or Sydney on cruises to the sun, before war disrupted the routine and the 'White Sisters' were conscripted for government service.

By the autumn of 1936 three of the 'White Sisters' were successfully in service and this photograph shows a particularly good view of the *Strathaird* at Circular Quay, Sydney. *(Author's Collection)*

The *Strathaird* at New Farm Wharf, Brisbane. She is obviously working cargo in Nos 1 and 2 holds. *(Author's Collection)*

Chapter Six

The Last 'White Sisters'

1936 was a very unsettled year, both at home and abroad, as the period of Appeasement began. At home the death of King George V meant that the throne passed to Edward VIII for his brief and turbulent reign, while in Europe the dictators were flexing their muscles as Mussolini pursued his quest for a new Roman Empire, and Hitler demonstrated his repudiation of the Treaty of Versailles by marching three battalions of his army into the demilitarized left bank of the Rhineland. It was his first test of French and British will which, sadly, was totally lacking. In Spain General Francisco Franco moved his army from Spanish Morocco to oust the hotchpotch of left wing organizations which formed the government in Madrid, thereby triggering the Spanish Civil War.

Initially the world tension proved to be a boon for the British shipbuilding industry with the announcement of the Royal Navy's biggest naval construction programme in 15 years and the placing of orders for 38 new warships. It was in this atmosphere that P&O placed orders with Vickers Armstrong of Barrow-in-Furness for two new vessels, yard numbers 722 and 723. They were to be very similar in design and appearance to the *Strathmore*, but they would also incorporate many features which were improvements on the original three *Straths*. Yard number 722 was christened *Stratheden* and was launched on Thursday 10 June 1937, a brilliantly sunny day at Walney Island which drew thousands of spectators to the shipyard and to the shores opposite. The vessel's sponsor was the Duchess of Buccleuch and Queensberry, who was a fitting choice, for one of the Duke's ancestors had been a pioneer of shipbuilding at Barrow. The new liner took her initial plunge at noon that day and she presented an imposing and dignified appearance as she floated in the sunlit channel, whilst busy tugs made ready to tow her

to the Buccleuch Dock for fitting out. At the luncheon which followed the ceremony, the political preoccupations of the day were touched upon by Alexander Shaw, who appealed for friendship between Britain and Germany.

Just under three months later, on Thursday 23 September 1937, the last of the five sisters took to the water. The ceremony was performed by the Countess of Cromer, who was accompanied by her husband, Lord Cromer, a member of the P&O Board. Once again the event was witnessed by thousands of spectators who, together with the official guests, '...cheered heartily as the *Strathallan* thundered down the slipway into her natural element.' The chairman of the P&O, who had by then inherited the family title and become Lord Craigmyle, again made an important national speech. This time the subject was the ever rising cost of shipbuilding in the British shipyards. He also referred to the 'rearmament phase' and spoke of when it would be over. Sadly it was to be eight years before that would come about.

The last two 'White Sisters' were similar in appearance to the *Strathmore*, with a straight stem, cruiser stern, well-proportioned single funnel and two pole masts. They had eight decks which were for the use of passengers and these were designated from the Boat Deck downwards, A to H, including the Promenade Decks. As the two ships were almost identical, a detailed description of the *Stratheden* will cover both. There was accommodation for 448 first class passengers in 216 single and 116 two-berth rooms on C, D and E Decks. There were also a few two-berth cabins forward of the dining saloon on F Deck. On D Deck there were two Viceregal Suites which comprised a dining-room, sitting-room, verandah, bedroom and bathroom. There were also six de luxe cabins on the same deck. A large number of the first class cabins had bathrooms attached and one innovation on

The *Stratheden* was launched on Thursday 10 June 1937, a warm, sunny day at Walney Island, Barrow-in-Furness. *(P&O)*

P&O ships was the installation of a telephone in each cabin, connected to a central exchange.

The first and tourist class public rooms of both the *Stratheden* and *Strathallan* were similar to those of the *Strathmore* in many respects, but they also showed several minor improvements, such as the introduction of lighter veneers and colour schemes. Although no traditional styles were used in the rooms, the creations were based on good contemporary designs and furnishing fabrics. The idea was to give full effect to the various woods used, many of which were 'Empire grown' and for the guidance of passengers the different woods in each room were identified on small notices at the entrances.

The first class dining saloon on F Deck was arranged to seat 260 passengers at tables for two, four, six and eight, and the restaurant service was claimed to be the best provided by the company at that time. The walls of the room were panelled in finely figured ash and chestnut with contrasting bands of Australian walnut and were decorated with mirrors

which, in their turn, were engraved and sandblasted with pleasing designs. There was a cold buffet forward and a sideboard aft, which were also incorporated into the decorative scheme and which formed the central features of the room. The deckhead over the central portion was raised by some 18 inches and it was illuminated by a central light fitting of a contemporary design. The remainder of the room was lit by similar fittings which, combined with wall brackets, gave very good lighting. The door grilles and window screens were finished in anodized aluminium which contrasted well with the woodwork. The windows were glazed in soft-tinted glass and in the evenings they were floodlit from behind. The deck was covered with what was described as light-coloured 'korkoid'. Adjacent to the foyer on the port side there was a children's dining-room, which seated 46 youngsters in small armchairs.

All the other first class public rooms were on B Deck and they were arranged *en suite*, so that the passengers had a clear view aft from the Library, through the entrance hall, Lounge,

This dramatic bow view shows the last of the five sisters, the *Strathallan*, as she plunges into the waters of the Walney Channel on 23 September 1937.

(P&O)

After her launch the *Strathallan* was berthed alongside the almost completed *Stratheden* in Buccleuch Dock.

(Vickers PLC)

Another view of the *Strathallan* and the *Stratheden* at the Vickers Armstrong shipyard.

(Vickers PLC)

The *Strathmore* alongside Adelaide's Outer Harbour on 12 July 1955. She left early the following day for Melbourne and Sydney.
(*Duncan Smedley*)

The *Strathaird* at Sydney in the late 1950s.

(*Don Smith*)

The *Stratheden* at anchor in Belfast Lough following her trials in the Clyde and during her voyage to Tilbury. The engineers were hard at work on a machinery fault which had developed. *(VSEL)*

dance space and Verandah Café. This gave an impressive feeling of space for the traveller on the long voyage to Australia. The Library with Writing Room was right forward beneath the bridge and the forward end determined the design of the decorative work, which was further emphasized by large bow windows to both port and starboard. This lofty room was panelled in figured weathered sycamore and walnut and the main feature was the elegant marble fireplace fitted with an electric radiant fire. On the panel above the fireplace there was a fine oil painting of St Paul's Cathedral by Norman Wilkinson. There was a parquet floor and the room could be converted into a cinema for 200 people with, in contemporary parlance, 'talkie apparatus'. Aft of the Library, across the spacious main entrance hall, access was gained to the Lounge through wide, glazed metalwork doors. This room was panelled in myrtle wood, with contrasting bandings of Australian walnut, and definite breaks were incorporated in the form of recessed niches in silver metal lit by long upright bracket fittings. The centre part had a raised ceiling which was reflected in a large mirror-glass panel at the forward end, and this gave the room a feeling of extraordinary spaciousness. At the after end there was a modern fireplace with an engraved mirror depicting an Assyrian lion hunt. The port and starboard wings of the room led aft to vestibules screened off with metal grilles, adjoining the dance area.

The dancing space was simply decorated in a shade of sunshine yellow with well-positioned light fixtures with special coloured lighting in the concealed trough of a raised central dome. The sides were composed of glazed and hinged screens which could be raised or lowered. Proceeding aft

again one entered the Verandah Café through small staircase vestibules on both the port and starboard sides. This took the place of what had been the Smoking Room on the earlier ships and it was a clear indication of the change in social trends. The café was panelled in finely figured and light-coloured betula veneer with contrasting peroba and elm burr, and metal enrichments in stainless steel. At the after end were three wide, folding screen doorways which led to the swimming-pool and which, when opened, made a 10 ft-wide space, a great asset in tropical weather. The pool itself was in a fine position aft of the Verandah Café and it was finished in a simple but effective manner in white, jade green and bright teak. Dressing cubicles were arranged to both port and starboard, with seating around the pool and ample sunbathing space. As on the earlier ships, the first class sports and games area was on A Deck, and at the after end this overlooked the lido area on B Deck below.

The tourist class passengers had three public rooms as well as a nursery and dining saloon arranged in the after section of the ship, and while they were neither as large nor as elaborate, they equalled the comfort of the first class. The dining saloon on F Deck extended throughout the ship's width and could accommodate 332 passengers in one sitting. The Smoking Room was on the same deck, while the Lounge and swimming-pool were on E Deck. Above this on D Deck there was a verandah and covered dance space. Promenades were provided on D, E and F Decks, with a large sports area on C Deck. The tourist class passengers were accommodated in cabins on F, G and H Decks.

One significant design improvement over the *Strathmore*

The last two 'White Sisters' were similar in appearance to the *Strathmore*. This view shows the *Strathallan*. *(Vickers PLC)*

was the fact that the first class swimming-pools were sited one deck higher, which released more deck space for first class passengers and allowed six more 'bathroom' cabins to be installed in each ship. It also allowed more space on C Deck for the tourist promenade, and the tourist dance space was considerably improved as it gained the area which would have been taken up by the swimming-pool tank. Another major improvement was the siting of more tourist cabins on G Deck with a reduction in the number on H Deck. In addition the single funnel on the new ships was some nine feet taller than that of the *Strathmore*, which assisted greatly with the problem of clearing funnel soot from the upper decks.

Like the *Strathmore*, the *Stratheden* and *Strathallan* were propelled by twin screws, each being driven by a set of Parsons turbines through single-reduction gearing. Each set comprised one high-pressure, one intermediate-pressure, and one low-pressure turbine, which worked in series and drove separate pinions which engaged with the main gearwheel. The steam generating installation consisted of six Babcock & Wilcox high-pressure marine boilers. There were four large and two small boilers which were fitted with superheaters and tubular air heaters. They burned oil under a forced draught system and supplied steam at 450psi and 725°F. In all the machinery developed 24,000 SHP and gave the ships a service speed of 21 knots.

After dry docking in Liverpool, the *Stratheden* ran her trials off the Isle of Arran between Friday 10 and Saturday 11 December 1937, in exceptionally severe weather conditions. The wind speeds varied between Force 6 and 8, and blizzards reduced the visibility to almost nil at times. However, despite this, on sights of three runs, when it was possible to see the mile posts, a mean speed of 21.8 knots was recorded. On Saturday evening the vessel anchored off Greenock and a number of Press representatives embarked for the voyage to Tilbury. Also on board were 200 workmen from Vickers' yards who were working day and night to complete the fitting out, and the deep booming of her siren in the fog dominated the sound of their hammers as the vessel left Greenock for her voyage down the Irish Sea. Soon after her departure, salt was detected in the boiler feed-water and so she anchored in Belfast Lough for over 24 hours, from early on 12 December until 2pm on the 13th, until the source of the leak could be traced. It was found to be in one of the auxiliary generators and as soon as the problem was rectified the ship proceeded without incident to Tilbury, where she was held up in the Thames Estuary for a number of hours due to fog. The *Stratheden* was handed over to the P&O Company on Wednesday 15 December 1937, soon after her arrival in the Thames, and Captain R. Harrison DSO RD RNR, who had left the *Strathmore* in the summer of 1937 to stand by the new ship and who was the Commodore of the fleet, took command.

It was another three months before the *Strathallan* was completed, and she was handed over to the company on 10 March 1938, two days before German troops crossed the border into Austria at the 'request' of Seyss-Inquart, the Austrian Chancellor. The clouds of war were thickening over Europe.

The *Stratheden's* first class Sports Deck, looking forward on the port side. *(Author's Collection)*

The *Stratheden's* first class Library and Writing Room which was situated at the forward end of B Deck. Norman Wilkinson's oil painting of St Paul's Cathedral can be seen between the bookcases. *(Author's Collection)*

The first class Lounge in the *Stratheden*. It had a feeling of extraordinary spaciousness. *(Author's Collection)*

The first class dining saloon in the *Stratheden* was on F Deck and it was arranged to seat 260 passengers at tables for two, four, six and eight.
(Author's Collection)

The tourist class Lounge in the *Stratheden*. Whilst it was neither as large nor as elaborate, the comfort equalled that of the first class equivalent. *(Author's Collection)*

The *Stratheden's* tourist class Smoking Room was at the after end of F Deck. *(Author's Collection)*

The first class Lounge in the *Strathallan* was on B Deck and it was entered by way of double swing doors in the main entrance foyer.

(National Museums & Galleries on Merseyside)

The main entrance foyer situated on the *Strathallan's* F Deck. This view is looking from port to starboard, and to the left of the photograph are the directions to first class cabins 15 to 41. To the right of the photograph is the main staircase, on either side of which were the entrances to the dining saloon.   *(National Museums & Galleries on Merseyside)*

Chapter Seven

The Uneasy Peace

As the last two 'White Sisters' neared completion at Barrow-in-Furness, the first three vessels continued to ply the trade route between London and Brisbane without any major problems. On 22 April 1937 the *Strathmore* unfortunately collided with the Ballard Pier at Bombay and suffered damage to her bow plating. She was immediately taken into dry dock, but luckily she was able to sail for London two days later with a large number of distinguished passengers on board, who were to be guests at the coronation of King George VI. She arrived in Southampton at midnight on Sunday 9 May 1937, three days before the coronation ceremony, to a hive of activity in the port. A large number of passenger liners arrived that weekend with visitors, and a number of ships returned from cruises which had been scheduled to end just before the coronation. The *Strathmore* was one of five large liners which had been chartered by the government in order to accommodate official guests, of which there were almost 3,000, for the Coronation Fleet Review which was held off Spithead on Thursday 20 May.* The *Strathmore* remained at Southampton in the ten days preceding the Review and on 19 May she embarked her passengers, before

Strathmore passes the cruiser HMS *Southampton* at the Royal Fleet Review in May 1937.   *(National Maritime Museum)*

steaming down Southampton Water to the Solent the next day.

With over 1,000 ships of all types and sizes assembled there, the Solent was a magnificent sight on the Thursday morning and hundreds of people had spent the night on Southsea Beach in order to get a good vantage point. The Review started at 3.05pm when, preceded by the Trinity House flagship *Patricia* and escorted by the Admiralty yacht *Enchantress,* the Royal Yacht *Victoria & Albert,* with the King and Queen aboard, left Portsmouth's South Railway Jetty. As she passed Southsea Castle, the Solent reverberated to the crash of a 21-gun salute and at 3.30pm the Royal Yacht, followed by the *Enchantress* and then the *Strathmore,* and the other four big liners, steamed westwards between D and F lines of battleships.

All the men-of-war were fully manned, with guards and bands paraded and three cheers were given as the *Victoria & Albert* passed by. At about 5.30pm, with the Review completed, the Royal Yacht returned between the line of foreign warships, which included the German pocket battleship, *Admiral Graf Spee,* and anchored at the head of F line. The *Strathmore* anchored close behind, almost parallel with the *Victoria & Albert,* just east of Horse Sand Fort. That evening passengers were treated to the sight of the fleet illuminated in a blaze of light and a spectacular firework display. On the following morning, with the fleet dispersing, the *Strathmore* steamed back into Southampton where the government guests disembarked and passengers embarked for a three-week Mediterranean cruise which started that evening.

The *Strathnaver* spent the summer season of 1937 cruising from London and Southampton, and her first Australian voyage after the last of her cruises got off to a bad start. As she left 31 berth in Tilbury Docks on Saturday 11 September, a strong gust of wind caught her and swung her stern into the quay, smashing an electrically driven crane on the dockside. Eventually the four tugs managed to manoeuvre her into the river where she was anchored in Gravesend Reach. After being examined by divers she was able to sail for Marseilles later that evening. During the voyage she made an unusual cruise from Sydney to Brisbane and Auckland.

On Christmas Eve 1937 the *Stratheden* left Tilbury for her maiden voyage to Brisbane and sailed from Marseilles on New Year's Day, 1938. It was the height of the season for the ships which travelled between the UK and Australia, and she was fully booked in both classes when she left the French port. She eventually arrived at New Farm Wharf in the Brisbane River on 7 February 1938, having received an enthusiastic welcome in all the Australian ports. She was on her return voyage, in the Red Sea between Aden and Suez, when her sister ship *Strathallan* left Tilbury on 18 March 1938 for her maiden voyage to Brisbane. The two ships were together in Marseilles, the first time they had met since the summer of 1937 at Barrow. At last the five 'White Sisters' were at sea, but they had only 18 months ahead of them plying their peacetime routes together before war would alter their roles

*The other ships being *Vandyck, Rangitiki, Laurentic,* and *Cameronia*

The *Strathnaver* in the Thames. She spent the summer season of 1937 cruising from London. *(Author's Collection)*

The *Stratheden* left Tilbury for her maiden voyage to Brisbane on 24 December 1937. Here she is shown at Sydney. *(Author's Collection)*

for over seven years.

Mr Len Wyeth of Lincolnshire recalls one voyage he made as an Assistant Purser in the *Strathaird* in early 1938, when they carried Mr & Mrs J. Logie Baird on board. They were travelling to Australia no doubt to acquaint the 'Aussies' with the miracle of television, and Len Wyeth recalls one of the great inventor's eccentricities when, during the ship's transit of the Red Sea, Mr Baird insisted on sleeping with two thick woollen blankets over him. In June 1938 Len Wyeth joined the *Strathmore*, again as an Assistant Purser, and he recalls his years on board this vessel with pleasure: 'This ship had the reputation of being a happy one and I found this to be true and this atmosphere prevailed throughout the war years.'

The *Strathallan* eventually arrived back in London from Australia on 24 June 1938 and during that summer she made three Mediterranean cruises and one to the Northern Capitals of Oslo, Stockholm and Copenhagen. George Shaw of Southend, who eventually retired from the P&O as a personnel manager, joined the *Strathallan* as a bellboy for her second Australian voyage which started from Tilbury on 16 September 1938. At the time European political tensions had reached new heights with Hitler's demands for the accession of the Sudetenland area of Czechoslovakia, and on the day before the *Strathallan* sailed, the British Prime Minister, Neville Chamberlain, had flown to Berchtesgaden to meet Hitler, and the Royal Navy had been placed in readiness for mobilization. However, Appeasement was at its height and Chamberlain's speech which included the famous words,

The *Strathallan* arrives in the River Thames watched by the crew of a Thames sailing barge.

(Vickers PLC)

'How horrible, fantastic, incredible it is that we should be digging trenches, trying on gas masks here because of a quarrel in a far away country between people of whom we know nothing', sums up the feeling of the times.

George Shaw signed on for a monthly wage of £3.4s.6d (£3.22½), from which he had to buy his uniforms, and reported on board to the Second Steward. The stewards' accommodation in the peak was full and he, together with about a dozen others, was berthed in converted passenger cabins in the tourist class section on H Deck. He recalls that, 'We boasted a porthole, but its low level above the water-line meant it had to be closed when any sort of sea was running. An added attraction was that we were adjacent to the trunking of a hold and between the steel stanchions one could see the dockers sweating and cursing when handling the cargo and mail. Very little time was allowed for the formalities of settling in and as it was embarkation day there was not much chance of seeing your bunk until very much later on. Embarkation took place in the afternoon with all hands turned to guiding passengers to their cabins and carrying their hand luggage for them. It was my first experience of being tipped, mostly sixpences from confused emigrants making their "voyage of a lifetime" in the tourist class, but there was sometimes half a crown. Then there were the telegrams, so much a feature of sailing day at that time, to be delivered to cabins, an exercise on which I spent much energy that first

time, because decks and cabins were still a mystery. It was "Munich time" and the farewells of those who had come to see their loved ones off were that much more poignant. It was not long before the first meal of the voyage was served and as the tourist class dining saloon filled up, it became alive to a level of babble and clatter which would last for the next month, when the last passengers disembarked at Brisbane.

My day started at 6.30am, when the night-watchman woke everybody and, after grabbing a cup of coffee, we "ticked on" with the Leading Steward. First trippers were usually allocated jobs aft in the tourist class where there were rosters for watching the bell-board in the pantry, operating the lifts, delivering the "wireless news", which had been typed on Gestetner skins and duplicated in the bureau, and fetching and carrying for dining saloon waiters. There were also stand-by duties at the bureau to deliver the Purser's messages to officers or passengers. The excitement of all this soon gave way to the effect of seasickness as the ship rounded Ushant and entered "the Bay". The awfulness of this had been smugly forecast by those who no longer suffered and an old Goan pantryman, who had seen my distress, guaranteed his "cure" – a pint of seawater and dry biscuits. I must have been the exception, because I endured a state of misery until the ship cleared Cape St Vincent. We were in and out of Gibraltar one morning, with snatched views of the grandeur of the Rock and after lunch we steamed into Tangier with the unforgettable

The *Strathallan* in the entrance lock of Tilbury Docks. This photograph was taken in March 1938, shortly after she had been handed over to P&O.
(Vickers PLC)

sight of the white buildings climbing up the hills from the shoreline. We did not go alongside and the few passengers who embarked and disembarked were handled by tender.

Our next port of call was Marseilles, where we went alongside and spent the night. Passengers taking advantage of the day and a half journey from London, instead of our four to five days' passage, came on board, along with the mail. The afternoon watch on the bell-board found all the bellboys at a low ebb and I had difficulty in not dozing off. One afternoon I answered a cabin bell and the occupant requested two "gimlets". At that time my knowledge of cocktails was very limited, and all I could think was that he had lost his baggage trunk keys. I made the mistake of waking the carpenter from his afternoon "kip" to ask for the only "gimlets" I knew of! Malta was our next port of call, where we were moored to a buoy in Grand Harbour alongside an Italian liner with a considerable number of troops on board, bound for Ethiopa.

Next was one of the "events" of the voyage, the Suez Canal transit. We went to buoys not far from the Canal Authority's offices and we were soon besieged with bumboats and a proliferation of Egyptian "Jock Mackenzies" who did their best to prise a few shillings from the novices. The *Strathallan* had a Canal searchlight built into the stem (behind the company crest), and so we did not require the unwieldy "box

arrangement" which was usually shipped at Port Said. There was still much activity however, with the embarkation of the Canal Pilot (who was held in some awe), sundry assistants and a large team of Egyptian "fellahs" with their boat brought inboard onto the fore well-deck. For most of the time they seemed to be in a state of repose in odd corners around the forecastle. Some passengers left to do sightseeing tours to Cairo and rejoined at Port Suez after our transit. During the slow passage south I strived to see as much as possible of the wave generated by the ship rushing along the canal bank and the scenic spots such as Ismailia and the Bitter Lakes. Within a day or two of our departure from Port Said we called at Port Sudan, a hot, dusty place and I have recollections of "fuzzy-wuzzies" carrying our cargo, including enormous crates on their backs, their spindly legs and mass of hair standing out as they staggered down the quay under a blazing sun. It was at this time that my left hand became infected and swollen and the Assistant Surgeon, in those days before antibiotics, decided to make an incision to deal with the problem. This coincided with the stifling heat of the Red Sea and I had to take a few days off duty. It gave me an opportunity to see a breath-taking view of Jeddah with its Arabic houses, which could be clearly seen as the ship went close in. We also saw a number of isolated islands, baking in the intense heat, their only occupants being lighthouse keepers.

The *Strathallan* off Gravesend. Vivid memories of the vessel's maiden voyage are recalled by George Shaw.

(Author's Collection)

Our next call was Aden (2 October 1938) with its seering heat, looking stark, burnt-out and barren. There were another lot of bumboats and this time I bought two Japanese-made silk shirts for 1/6d each (7¹/₂p). "Wait until we clear the Gulf of Aden and the weather will be cooler", said the pundits, and thankfully they were right, but our arrival in Bombay coincided with the onset of the monsoon weather with torrential rain and uncomfortable humidity. We berthed at Ballard Pier, the ship being assisted by some noisy tugs, and this was the port where a significant number of first class passengers disembarked to take up the reins of the "white man's burden" after home leave. Passenger trains with such glamorous names as the "Frontier Mail" were waiting for those going up-country, with a mass of porters to transfer the baggage. Milling crowds were everywhere and there was much excitement amongst our Indian crew, who were now in their home port. They were from a variety of religions, Catholic Goan stewards and Hindu Lascars on deck, in their neat blue uniforms and distinctive headwear. I was becoming increasingly aware of their titles such as, Serangs, Tindals, Cassabs and Bhandaries. The engine-room crew were Muslims with baggy-trousered uniforms and names such as Ogwallahs and Paniwallahs. However, despite the bedlam of Bombay there was an air of timelessness about it. After a couple of days steaming we arrived at Colombo, where a relaxed atmosphere prevailed and during the afternoon I walked out of town to some botanical gardens where exotic plants and wildlife abounded.

Our departure from Colombo signalled the longest sea passage of the voyage, nine days to Fremantle, which was broken only by a diversion to the Cocos Islands, where there was a wireless station and it was customary for P&O ships to drop a barrel of mail and supplies overboard. Two or three boats were there to meet us and we all gazed down on them, while the occupants seemed to be willing us to stay. All we could give them were a couple of engine movements to provide them with a lee and drop their barrel, which drifted astern as the *Strathallan* slowly manoeuvred ahead. Soon after

A rare view of the *Strathnaver* and the *Strathaird* in Sydney Harbour on 28 November 1936. The *Strathaird* was leaving the port for Brisbane on the last leg of her outward voyage and the *Strathnaver* was bound for Melbourne and then London, via Suez.

(Laurence Sanderson)

45

we left Colombo we crossed the Equator, but I cannot recall any special event to mark the occasion, perhaps I was too busy to notice. There seemed to be a more relaxed air with the prospect of the long sea passage, and one of the bellboys' jobs was to attend to clearing up the first class lounge, where dancing went on until about 11pm. One of the favourites was the Lambeth Walk and I recall the Purser, Mr Aries, performing the dance particularly well. There was little in the way of organized entertainment, although the tourist class had an occasional film on deck and it was possible to sneak a view from behind the canvas screens which were rigged up. I also became aware that the *Strathallan* was up to date with the latest technology, having air-conditioning in the first class dining saloon and telephones, complete with main switchboard, for the first class cabins.

There was an air of expectancy as we made landfall off Australia and docked at Fremantle (18 October 1938), and after leaving that port we were at sea for three days before arriving at Adelaide. From there we went to Melbourne, but Sydney was our main port of call where, on 27 October, we went alongside Circular Quay, in the shadow of the Harbour Bridge which, at that time, had not long been opened. It was an irresistible attraction to walk across and I lost no time in doing so, and for a few pence I got a ferry to Manly Beach. On our arrival in Brisbane I went to make a call on a friend of my mother and the address, I remember, was Lower River Terrace. I recall asking directions from some men who were digging a hole in the road, and they showed considerable interest in where I was from and they continually addressed me as "Pommy". I remember the friend giving me a wonderful welcome. I was entertained with an enormous meal, followed by a trip in an ancient car to the countryside outside the city.

We retraced our voyage back to Tilbury and I remember there was much concern at the imminence of war, and in addition to the usual boat drill we had exercises in "blacking-out" the ship. We finally berthed at Tilbury on 23 December 1938 and I paid off with over £11 in wages. Two large white "fivers", their numbers duly recorded, were handed to me and I felt rich that Christmas.'

George Shaw returned to the *Strathallan* after a ten-day period of leave and he made the vessel's third Australian voyage which began on 20 January 1939. He was promoted to Kitchen Clerk, with a wage of £4.8s.9d (approximately £4.44) a month, and this job entailed taking orders from cabin stewards on behalf of passengers who, for one reason or another, could not get to the dining saloon. Other tasks involved checking the stores which were delivered daily to the galley and delivering summaries of the weekly 'bar chits' to all officers. He recalls that one important fringe benefit was being able to eat in the galley from the first class menu rather than in the crew's mess with unattractive fare. On this voyage, instead of the usual long stop-over in Sydney, the *Strathallan* made a cruise to New Zealand, calling at Auckland and Wellington before returning to Tilbury on 28 April 1939. After undergoing maintenance at Tilbury she left the port on 11 May of that fateful year for a 19-day cruise into the Mediterranean, which took her to Gibraltar, Alexandria and Malta, arriving back in Tilbury on 30 May and ten days later, on 9 June 1939, she left London on her final peacetime voyage to Brisbane. Following the Munich Agreement there was a relaxing of tension on the European political scene although, as events were to prove, this was only a temporary lull and events ground on inexorably towards the Second World War.

A magnificent view of the *Strathaird* at night. This was taken during a Mediterranean cruise in the late 1930s.

(Laurence Sanderson)

Chapter Eight

War Comes To Europe

In July 1939 tensions in Europe were once more on the boil and this time it was over the League of Nations city of Danzig. In fact Hitler had already secretly declared to his generals his intention of invading Poland, and Britain and France had offered, '...total and unqualified support to Poland in the event of any action which clearly threatened Polish independence, and which the Polish government accordingly considered it vital to resist with their national forces.' This agreement caused Hitler to postpone the invasion of Poland, whilst he concentrated his country's efforts on reaching a neutrality agreement with Russia, and as these momentous events were played out in Europe the ships of the P&O continued to ply their peaceful trade routes to India, Australia and the Far East.

The *Strathnaver* arrived back in London from Brisbane on 26 May 1939 and she then undertook a 16-day Mediterranean cruise before leaving for Australia once again on 7 July. It was her last pre-war voyage and she arrived in Brisbane on 20 August 1939, leaving two days later for a cruise which took her to Rabaul in Papua New Guinea. She called at the port on 26 August and with the political crisis in Europe coming to a head, she made a dramatic return to Sydney which is recalled here by Lieutenant-Commander John de Broughton, who was a cadet aboard her: 'I remember vividly when war did come. We were on our way back from Rabaul to Sydney. I was sent down to the captain's cabin to deliver an important message and there he was stretched out in his bed, complete with bed socks and a nightcap. As a result of this message we immediately darkened ship and increased speed to the maximum 21 knots, but this soon fell back to the usual 18 knots as the engines could not take the strain. We arrived at Circular Quay on 31 August and we

were there when war was declared. The crew immediately went over the side and painted the white hull and yellow funnels a uniform grey. From the depths of No 6 hold two packing cases emerged, containing an ancient 6-inch gun and an almost as ancient 3-inch high-angle gun, which were duly mounted on pre-positioned fittings on the poop. Whilst these ancient weapons created a very loud noise and certainly shook up the whole ship, it is doubtful whether they were of much practical use against the enemy. Our schedule was somewhat altered for the return passage and we finally docked at Liverpool, instead of London, on 19 October 1939.'

As soon as she docked, work began to convert the *Strathnaver* for her wartime role of a troop transport, a function which all the 'White Sisters' would eventually fulfil. A great proportion of her cabin furniture, particularly in the tourist class, was taken out and the bulkheads between the cabins were dismantled. Huge troop mess-decks fitted with hammocks and long mess-tables were installed, together with small metal kit lockers. Both dining saloons were converted into mess-decks and additional bunks were fitted into all the remaining cabins. The first class lounge was converted into the officers' dining-room and the Verandah Café became a warrant officers' mess. Within a matter of a few weeks the conversion was finished, but much of the work was rushed and there was a great deal of improvisation. Work continued right up to the moment on 10 November 1939 when she sailed round to London and then left for Australia again, steaming via Suez, Bombay and Colombo and arriving in Sydney on 4 January 1940.

Meanwhile, the *Strathnaver*'s sister ship *Strathaird* had left London on 12 May 1939 for a routine voyage to Brisbane, where she arrived on 25 June. Two days later she left the port

The *Strathaird*, having been fitted out as a troopship, lies in Tilbury Docks in October 1939.

(Alex Duncan)

The *Strathallan* on her arrival at Cape Town on 15 September 1939, having been diverted from her normal route through the Mediterranean. *(Charles Lowe)*

During her six-day stop in Cape Town the *Strathallan* received her grey 'warpaint'. In this view the white hull is rapidly disappearing. *(Charles Lowe)*

and arrived back at Tilbury Landing Stage at 8am on Friday 18 August 1939. She was due to sail once more for Brisbane on 6 September, but on 28 August, ten days after her arrival in London, it was announced that this voyage was cancelled. She was requisitioned by the government and she too was fitted out as a troopship. She left Tilbury, commanded by Captain D.M. Stuart, on 29 August 1939 bound for the Clyde where she embarked troops and then sailed for Suez, by way of the Mediterranean, before continuing to Aden and Cape Town and returning to Tilbury on 11 November 1939 after calling at Takoradi and Freetown in West Africa.

The *Strathmore* sailed from London to Brisbane, her final peacetime Australian voyage, on 14 April 1939 and arrived back at Tilbury on 21 July. After 13 days in her home port she left on a 14-day cruise to Stockholm and Copenhagen on 4 August, returning to Southampton at 8am on Friday 18 August. On the next day she sailed on a cruise to the Mediterranean and, after calling at Gibraltar and Casablanca,

she was steaming east for Alexandria when she was recalled to London. Although it was announced officially that her itinerary had been altered to take her to Bermuda and the Azores, she returned direct to Tilbury. Mr G.L. Jones of Southampton, who had joined the ship as Fourth Engineer on 4 August that year, recalls that after being ordered home the voyage was made under black-out conditions, '...a taste of things to come.' She arrived in Tilbury Docks on 29 August and she was lying there when war was declared. Mr Jones recalls: 'Just after the fateful broadcast on 3 September, the air raid warning sounded and all the engineers were ordered below to prepare the vessel for instant departure, but fortunately it was a false alarm.' Whilst she was in Tilbury she was painted grey and she left again on 15 September 1939 for a routine sailing to Sydney, by way of Gibraltar, Malta, Suez, Aden, Colombo and the usual Australian ports. After a safe passage to Australia she returned via the same route to Southampton on 5 December 1939, before sailing once more

The *Strathallan* with her grey hull, funnel and superstructure almost completed, lies alongside the wharf at Cape Town. *(Charles Lowe)*

21 September 1939, and the now battleship-grey *Strathallan*, with a 6-inch gun at her stern, is about to leave Cape Town for Tilbury.
(Alex Duncan)

for a passenger voyage to Sydney, again via the Mediterranean, on Boxing Day that year. Len Wyeth recalls that there were quite a number of evacuee children on board and he, together with other officers, used to read them bedtime stories. He also recalls rumours of a U-boat in the Bay of Biscay, and whether this was true or not he never found out, but as the ship steamed through the Mediterranean and as the weather got hotter, the passengers were allowed to sleep on deck for, with the strict black-out in force and all portholes and deadlights shut, conditions became very uncomfortable below. He recalls that women and children slept on one side of the deck and men on the other. He remembers that there were also a large number of German passengers on board, fugitives from Nazi Germany who were starting a new life in Australia. At Fremantle immigration and military security officers were embarked, and they interviewed the Germans at great length during the passage along the south coast of Australia and up the east coast. The *Strathmore* returned safely to the UK on 15 March 1940, during the 'Phoney War' period, and on 27 April, as the Norwegian campaign was being fought, she sailed for Australia once again by way of Suez. Upon her arrival in Sydney she was taken into the naval dockyard at Garden Island where some work was carried out to convert her for use as a troop transport. Once again the whole of the tourist class accommodation was stripped out and replaced by large, open troop mess-decks. She returned to Liverpool via the Cape in July 1940 and further work was carried out to fit her out for trooping. After this she left Liverpool on 14 August 1940 and she began trooping in earnest on the first of her long six-month voyages to Australia and the Middle East.

The latter end of May 1939 found the *Stratheden* leaving London for a series of cruises, the first of which took her to Dubrovnik, Trieste and Venice and back to Southampton on 12 June. The second 14-day cruise took her north to Reykjavik and Leith and this was followed by a cruise to Athens and Malta. Next she sailed on 28 July for Madeira, Dakar and Casablanca, and her last cruise also started in Southampton with an itinerary which included the Mediterranean ports of Piraeus, Rhodes and Malta. She arrived back in Tilbury at 3am on Monday 28 August 1939 and she was scheduled to sail for Australia on 1 September, just four days later. She did sail as planned and according to her Deputy Purser, Mr R.C. Temple of Hythe: 'Down Channel, in the dark, we hit some underwater wreckage whilst in the Downs. At the time it was rumoured to be a submarine and when we docked in Sydney there was a 60ft score on the underwater hull.* There was a full passenger list, with many people returning home to Australia and New Zealand and the black-out on board was a great novelty. We were delayed at Gibraltar until the situation in the Mediterranean became more clear and it was established that Italy was not joining the war immediately. Most of us on board, and particularly some Jewish refugees, were happy to clear Suez and steam into the Red Sea, and after we had left Colombo the black-out was lifted, for the last time until 1945.'

The newest of the 'White Sisters', the *Strathallan*, arrived in Brisbane on 23 July 1939 and left two days later for her return voyage to London. She arrived in Aden on 30 August, only four days before the declaration of war and two days before the German army slammed into Poland from Silesia, East Prussia and Slovakia. In those last, tense hours before the outbreak of war, Italy was an unknown quantity and it was not known whether Mussolini would declare war on Britain and France. As there were huge concentrations of the Italian armed forces in the Ethiopian province of Eritrea, which included submarines at Massawa (Mits 'iwa), it was decided to delay the *Strathallan* at Aden. Mr George Milne, who was a Junior Electrical Officer, recalls those days: 'Being berthed in Aden, which was known as the "cinder pot" and which King George V had described as, "one of the far-flung outposts of Empire, which hadn't been flung far enough", with the temperature well into the 90s gave us little comfort, and being there when the outbreak of war was announced, added to our depression. Our stay in Aden was spent blacking-out the ship.'

The *Strathallan* left Aden on 31 August 1939 and after steaming for six hours into the Red Sea she returned to the port. George Milne recalls that this exercise was carried out on more than one occasion before she finally left for Cape Town on 2 September. Three other ships joined her for the journey south, one of these being the ill-fated *City of Benares*. She arrived in the South African port on 15 September and left six days later, after having been painted grey, and finally arrived back in Tilbury on 9 October. Seventeen days later, on 26 October 1939, she left London once again for a normal mail voyage to Sydney and she was able to sail via the Mediterranean and return the same way to Southampton, where she arrived on 18 January 1940.

By the end of 1939 the *Strathnaver* and *Strathaird* were both on government service as troopships and the *Strathmore* and *Stratheden* were both requisitioned in the spring of 1940, although it was October 1940 before the *Strathallan* was taken over by the government and all the 'White Sisters' were in service as troop transports.

Following her conversion, the *Strathnaver* left the UK for Australia on 26 November 1939 and she was followed 15 days later by the *Strathaird,* which steamed across the Tasman Sea to New Zealand where she embarked troops in Wellington. On 10 January 1940, the *Strathnaver*, together with four Orient Line ships which included the *Orcades, Orford* and *Otranto,* were berthed at Pyrmont in Sydney. They had all embarked Australian troops for the Middle East and when they slowly pulled away from their berths that morning crowds of people packed onto every vantage point to cheer them off. As they passed under the Harbour Bridge hundreds of small craft followed the ships as they moved down the harbour towards the Heads, where thousands more people had gathered to add to the send-off. That afternoon the *Strathnaver* and her convoy rendezvoused with the *Strathaird* and her convoy of four ships carrying the New Zealand contingent. The ten troop transports, under the escort of four warships, sailed via Fremantle and transited the Suez Canal to disembark the troops at Suez. The *Strathaird* then returned to Sydney and Melbourne where she embarked more Australian troops for the Middle East. After disembarking

---

*In fact the incident happened at 9pm on 1 September and a survey at Gibraltar found that, not only was the underwater hull badly scored, but there was a slight leakage of sea water at the keel plate rivets. The surveyors stated the cause to have been a collision with sunken wreckage.

The *Strathnaver*, together with four Orient Line ships, left Sydney on 10 January 1940 with troops for the Middle East. This view shows the *Strathnaver* and the *Orcades* leaving the port. *(P&O)*

The *Stratheden*, with her hull and funnel painted black, is seen here at Singapore's Keppel Harbour during April 1940. *(P&O)*

these soldiers at El Kantara in the Suez Canal, she set course west through the Mediterranean, one of the last ships to use this route before it was closed to Allied shipping. As she left Port Said, the long-awaited German onslaught in Belgium, Holland and France began and on 29 May 1940, the day that the *Strathaird* arrived in Liverpool, the Germans occupied Ypres, Ostend and Lille. As soon as she arrived in the north-western port, work began on a major refit to prepare the ship for her demanding role which lay ahead. However, within two weeks the French army was rapidly collapsing and on 13 June 1940, the day before German troops marched into Paris, Captain R.C. Dene was ordered to get the *Strathaird* to sea without delay. She steamed south from the Mersey and called at Swansea, where orders were received that she should proceed to Brest to assist in the final evacuation from France. However, off Ushant she was diverted to Quiberon further down the coast. As there were no charts on board for this area, she was escorted by a British destroyer and, almost as soon as she had anchored, she was again ordered to Brest. For almost 12 hours on 17 June she lay at anchor off the port while troops and civilians poured on board. Time was short for this was the day when France sued for peace. In the event she embarked nearly 6,000 troops, 200 civilians, (which included children), cadets from a military academy in Brest and gold from British banks in Paris. The danger of the situation is illustrated by the sinking of the *Lancastria* at St Nazaire that same day, with the loss of thousands of lives. However, everything went well for the *Strathaird* and after

disembarking her passengers in Plymouth on 18 June she arrived back in Liverpool once again on 26 June 1940, the day after fighting in France ended.

The *Strathmore's* trooping career began in earnest on 13 August 1940 when she left Liverpool and sailed for Bombay via Cape Town and Mombasa and from there to the usual Australian ports. These were long voyages, and the ship did not return to Liverpool until 2 February 1941. Her next voyage kept her away from home for five months and took her to unusual ports such as Port Elizabeth in South Africa, Trinidad in the West Indies and Halifax, Nova Scotia.

The *Strathallan* made a mail voyage to Australia, leaving Southampton on 17 February 1940 and sailing via Marseilles, Malta and Suez. She arrived in Sydney just before the end of March that year and after a ten-day stop-over she left for Southampton once again. On 12 April 1940, off Fremantle, she passed the *Queen Mary* which was on a voyage from Cape Town to Sydney. As the *Strathallan* returned home via the Mediterranean, she made her final call at Marseilles on 8 May and arrived back in Southampton on 16 May 1940.

The newest of the five 'White Sisters' made only one more mail voyage to Australia, this time sailing via Cape Town and returning via the Sunda Straits and calling at Singapore for six days of maintenance in August. She arrived back in Liverpool on 6 October 1940 and over the next six weeks she too underwent an extensive refit and conversion for carrying troops.

The *Stratheden*, now painted grey, is seen at sea during the Second World War. Her 6-inch gun can be seen at the stern.   *(Maritime Photo Library)*

Chapter Nine

Troopin'

The year 1941 saw Britain standing alone against Nazi Germany and Italy, and in January that year the main action was in North Africa where British and Australian forces captured Tobruk and took 25,000 Italian prisoners. With the Mediterranean Sea closed, the troopships had to make their voyages to Egypt, which was the British base, via Cape Town. Another factor was the German occupation of northern France, and the air and U-boat threat to British shipping meant long voyages out into mid-Atlantic before turning south. All the south and east coast British ports were closed to the large troopships and instead they used Liverpool and the River Clyde.

The *Strathaird* had put in to Glasgow at the end of February 1941 for a refit and on completion of this she went down river to Gourock where a large troop convoy was forming up. She was commanded by Captain H. Williams, and at about 9pm on 24 March 1941 she cleared the entrance boom of the River Clyde. All the ships were steaming in single line ahead on a dark, foggy night, and the *Strathaird* was astern of the 25,000-ton Union Castle ship *Stirling Castle*. It was the largest troop convoy which had sailed from the Clyde, with 23 troopships, all of them large passenger liners. The P&O Company was represented by four ships, the *Strathaird, Strathnaver, Strathmore* and *Viceroy of India*, and they were bound for the Middle East and India. According to Mr Patrick Miles of Upton-upon-Severn, who was the Fourth Officer on board: 'We were steaming in single line ahead and in fog. We hadn't taken up our convoy formation and we couldn't have got any further than Ailsa Craig at very slow speed, when we hit the stern of the *Stirling Castle*.' With her bow quite seriously damaged, the voyage was abandoned and the *Strathaird* returned to the Clyde for repairs. Very few of the troops on board were even aware of the mishap. According to one of the gunners in 57 L.A.A. Regiment: 'We had two bofors guns mounted on the Boat Deck, but our hammocks were slung on H Deck, below the water-line. As far as we were concerned it was a quiet night, but when dawn broke we were surprised to find ourselves clear of the convoy and alone on a wide sea. We had breakfast and, as we were cleaning the guns, noticed land ahead. As we had expected to be in mid-Atlantic this was, to say the least, unexpected. To our greater surprise, an hour later there was land on either bow and eventually we found ourselves steaming up the Clyde. During the night the *Strathaird* and the ship immediately ahead, the *Stirling Castle,* had bumped and a good ten foot of *Strathaird's* bow was stoved in. We returned to Glasgow and the troops went ashore and on leave, leaving us gun teams to look after the bofors guns. *Strathaird* lay for a month at Glasgow, during which time the city was bombed.'

The *Strathaird* finally sailed from the Clyde on 26 April 1941 and once again the story is taken up by the ship's gunner: 'In April we joined another convoy to the Middle East. This time the voyage went as planned and three days into the Atlantic we turned for Freetown, Durban and Mombasa, then to Port Said. Round the Cape we hit a fair old storm which dispersed the convoy. One soldier was swept overboard and lost. We were unable to tend the guns and we lost a spare barrel which, in its 10-foot box slid overboard. From the anti-aircraft point of view the voyage was calm. Only one enemy aircraft was sighted, off Africa. The only firing practice we had was in the Red Sea, and this broke electric lights in a cabin on the deck below. We also had a couple of dirty barrels to clean.' On her return voyage the *Strathaird* crossed the Atlantic and called at Trinidad and Belize. At the latter port Patrick Miles recalls: 'We took on about 1,000 black loggers, big husky men from the mahogany forests. They were bound for the fir plantations in Scotland, which they must have found very cold in the winter.' In fact the ship returned to the Clyde on 23 August 1941, so the cold would not have been an immediate problem. Upon her return she was once again in dockyard hands and this time the refit lasted for three months.

She left the Clyde on 30 November 1941, commanded by Captain H. Williams, and once again she steamed to Suez via Cape Town. However, soon after leaving the Scottish port, the United States were plunged into the war after the Japanese attack on Pearl Harbor. So, on the homeward leg of the voyage she recrossed the Atlantic and called at Trinidad and New York. Once into the latter port the US authorities insisted that the vessel be fumigated, and so all her ship's company were accommodated ashore in hotels whilst this was carried out. Patrick Miles recalls that: 'It was another opportunity to do a bit of shopping, without the restrictions of rationing. On leaving we were commodore ship in a convoy which carried the first contingent of American troops to the UK, and we were accompanied by the battleship USS *Texas*. It was very rough weather for most of the crossing and the *Texas*, being rather round, rolled like nothing on earth. I'm sure she would have been quite useless in the event of an attack.' Fortunately this was never put to the test and she disembarked her US troops in Belfast before steaming into Liverpool on 28 January 1942.

The New Year of 1941 saw the *Strathallan* in Port Said and after an 11-day stay she left for Cape Town and eventually Gourock, where she arrived on 25 February that year. Two weeks later she sailed for Suez, and on the return voyage a mine was spotted in the Red Sea. This gave the ship's gunners some target practice and they blew it up with some good shooting. Like the *Strathaird*, the *Strathallan* crossed the Atlantic to call at Trinidad before setting course for Glasgow.

Life for the troops on all the converted liners during the Second World War was uncomfortable and the *Straths* were no exception. The mess-decks were very overcrowded and only a small proportion of the men were allowed on the upper decks at any one time, which limited their opportunity for exercise and recreation. They slept 'cheek by jowl' in their hammocks and toilet facilities were very limited; sometimes men had to negotiate as many as six decks in order to answer a call of nature. The food supply was also a problem with the

The *Strathmore* alongside Princes Landing Stage at Liverpool during the Second World War. The five *Straths* became regular callers at the port during the war.
(P&O)

The *Strathnaver* in late 1941 forming up with a troop convoy.
(Imperial War Museum)

ships carrying three or four times their peacetime complements, so there were no set mealtimes but a continuous cafeteria system with a monotonous menu was laid on instead. Strict water rationing had to be enforced and during long periods at sea this became very acute. Mr F. J. Smith of Felixstowe recalls a voyage he made in the *Strathaird* whilst serving with the RAF: 'There she stood, the *Strathaird*, our home for what was to be the next four weeks, although we did not know that at the time as we had not been told of our destination. It seemed that an endless stream of troops came aboard and that evening we set sail to the strains of a military band. The holds had been converted into mess and sleeping quarters, with hammocks slung at convenient points. Meals were from "hay boxes" brought by the duty orderly. The hammocks took some getting used to for a non sea-dog, but after some practice one found oneself in and out in a flash. We headed down the Irish Sea and out into the Atlantic and boat drill took place every day while the captain did his rounds with the duty officer - a white-gloved hand running along ledges searching for dirt. The mornings were mostly taken up cleaning the mess-deck, washing and boat drill, while the afternoons were taken up with card schools and the like. The toilets consisted of long metal troughs divided by wooden partitions with no doors. A constant flow of water ran through the troughs and it could be a hazardous occupation as certain practical jokers would light newspaper and float it down the trough. One can imagine men bobbing up along the line as the paper passed the nude posteriors.'

Captain J.A. Clifford of Pinner joined the *Stratheden* in Glasgow and recalls: 'The first thing one noticed in wartime Britain with its rationing was the variety and quantity of the food on board. There were four of us apprentices, all serving our time learning our trade as deck officers. In those days our parents had to pay £48 to the company for this privilege and this covered a three-year period. However, we were paid £5 a month, which rose to £10 a month after the first year at sea. We set off, I remember, from the Tail of the Bank in convoy with other troopships, bound for Bombay. We were heavily escorted to Freetown, after which we had fewer escorts. From there the convoy proceeded to Takoradi and Lagos and then to Cape Town. We remained in this land of plenty for a few days and the inhabitants were kind and friendly and most hospitable. Then, still in convoy, we rounded the Cape of Good Hope on an uneventful voyage to Bombay, where we stayed for ten to 14 days. During the voyage the ship carried in the region of 5,000 troops of all colours and description, male and female, army, navy and air force, a real mixed bag. The conditions on board for the troops were far from good. The original cabin accommodation had been removed to make way for large dormitories, and even some of the cargo space 'tween decks had been converted to troop accommodation. The washing and toilet facilities were poor and one can imagine the heat and stench in the tropics, even with what was, in those days, considered to be modern ventilation in a ship built for tropical voyages. It was, of course, made worse as the ship was blacked-out during the hours of darkness. The crew numbered between 600 and 700, consisting of British officers, petty officers and leading hands. In addition there were Indian seamen and firemen, and Goanese stewards. All very loyal and excellent seafarers to sail with.'

Despite these trying conditions, both crew members and troops alike coped well and only on rare occasions did anyone step out of line.

Anne Scott, then Anne Kennaway, returned home from South Africa in the *Stratheden*. She and her family had survived the sinking of the Orient liner *Orcades* in October 1942, and memories of that ordeal were fresh in their minds: 'We left Cape Town on 17 April 1943, travelling in convoy with another large passenger ship and escorted by a large warship, (MV *Britannic* and HMS *Warspite*). The ship itself was not in bad condition, it was full to capacity with troops and families. Some people were coming back from India to wartime Britain. There was a Lady Lumley, from Bombay, with her children and a Mrs Blandy with her daughter (my age). I shared a small, two-berth inner cabin, on the same side of the corridor as the bathrooms, with Henrietta du Boulay, whose husband was a POW in Singapore. Although bugs crawled out of the woodwork and bit us, I don't remember being particularly concerned. Most cabins were bug-free, it was a question of luck. The staff were always helpful and the food was not awful. The journey seemed very long and tedious and I was impatient to get back to the UK. There was one stop at Freetown, where I remember gazing with frustration at the little port and longing to go ashore and break the monotony, but no passengers were allowed off the ship. We must have travelled right in the middle of the South Atlantic, then the North Atlantic. First the weather was very hot, then it became cold and very rough. On 7 May there was an "alarm" when we all put on our life-jackets and went to boat stations. Thankfully not for long, it was an unidentified aircraft. We landed in Scotland on 10 May, having steamed up the Firth of Clyde to Gourock. Disembarking took a long time, standing in a queue all morning. We had no passports as they had been lost on the *Orcades*, but we were eventually able to get on the train which took 15 hours, and in the early morning of 11 May we arrived in London.'

The family had been evacuated from Singapore in early 1942, which gives some idea of the wartime difficulties for travellers.

Operation Torch

Early 1942 saw some serious set-backs for the Allies, particularly in the Far East where the British garrison of 90,000 troops surrendered at Singapore in what has been described as the 'greatest disaster to befall British arms', and the American forces on the Philippines surrendered to the Japanese. As the Japanese army advanced into Burma and their air force raided the British naval base at Trincomalee, the Indian Ocean became very dangerous for Allied shipping. At the highest level it was decided that the maximum Anglo-American effort would be put into the defeat of Germany, and with the political pressure for a second front it was clear that the Allies would have to take the initiative in Europe. All through 1942 the action in North Africa with the British and Commonwealth forces on the one hand and the German and Italian forces on the other, seemed to sway first one way and then the other. In the autumn of 1942 it was decided that there would be a decisive Allied effort to finish the North African campaign, which would be a prelude to an invasion of Italy. A landing in the Vichy-held countries of Algeria and Morocco was not without its dangers, for it could quite easily have bogged the Allies down in a campaign similar to Gallipoli in the First World War, which has been described as

'a conflict in the wrong place, at the wrong time and against the wrong enemy'. The Allies' objectives were to deny the control of West Africa to the Axis Powers and to provide a base for the eventual operations against southern Europe. The invasion itself was code-named 'Operation Torch' and there were three separate assault points for the invading forces. The western task force was to land in Morocco, the central task force at Oran, with Algiers the landing place for the eastern task force.

All five of the *Strath* liners would take part in the invasion and, sadly, only four of them would emerge from this vital Allied operation. All of the ships had been worked hard during 1942, mainly transporting troops to Egypt and India, but in March that year the *Strathallan* had made the hazardous voyage from Colombo to Fremantle, across the Indian Ocean. After calling at the Australian ports of Adelaide and Sydney she crossed the Tasman Sea to Auckland and then returned to Glasgow by way of the Panama Canal. Her next departure from the Clyde was at the end of May 1942 and after her usual voyage to Suez she returned via New York and Halifax, Nova Scotia. On this return journey she carried a large number of German POWs, and Mr Patrick

An aerial view of the first of the fast 'Torch' convoys. The *Strathnaver*, to the right of the picture, heads a column.

(Imperial War Museum)

Troops taking part in PT exercises on board the *Stratheden en route* to the 'Torch' landings in November 1942. They appear to be on B Deck between the Verandah Café and the swimming-pool.

(Imperial War Museum)

Here troops exercising on board the *Stratheden*, *en route* to the 'Torch' landings, are on the first class Sports Deck viewed from the starboard side looking aft. Compare this with the peacetime photograph in Chapter Six. (*Imperial War Museum*)

Italian POWs embarking on board the *Stratheden* at Algiers on 2 December 1942.

(Imperial War Museum)

Miles recalls that, 'These were a very different bunch to the usual Italian POWs as, while we were proceeding down the Mocambique Channel unescorted, they made a serious attempt to take over the ship by cutting up strips of ventilating shafts to make into weapons. Fortunately they were discovered by the army permanent staff and they were finally disembarked at Durban with a sigh of relief.'

After the entry of the USA into the war the *Strathnaver* carried US troops to Europe and Mr E. J. Read of Ringwood can recall that, upon leaving New York the ship was found to have oil in the feed-water supply and it was thought to have been an act of sabotage. He remembers that the ship, together with her complement of several thousand GIs, put into St John's, Newfoundland, for three weeks in order that repairs could be carried out. He remembers it as, '...a misty, damp place, made worse by having a ship full of GIs, and the three weeks felt like years.'

Captain D.G.O. Baillie was appointed as Staff Captain of the *Stratheden* in the autumn of 1942 and he joined the ship, which was commanded by Captain A.W. Drew, at Liverpool. He recalls that it was clear that something big was brewing as troopship after troopship came into the port and, after disembarkation, were reprovisioned but did not sail again. Extra guns were fitted to the *Stratheden* and the other ships and in early October she was ordered to Loch na Keal on the west side of the Island of Mull, where she lay at anchor for three weeks. According to Captain Baillie the loch was 'utterly desolate' and at night they had great difficulty in taking anchor bearings, '...for not a single light broke the general blackness, and since it deluged unremittingly with rain, we seldom had even the feeble assistance of the stars.'

On 26 October 1942, the *Strathnaver,* commanded by Captain E.M. Coates, left the Clyde as commodore ship at the head of a large convoy which consisted of 39 transports, together with 12 escorts. They steamed south-east into mid-Atlantic, before turning south in the direction of the Azores and eventually curving south-east for the Straits of Gibraltar. The voyage was uneventful until 5.30am on 7 November 1942, when a submarine torpedoed the US transport *Thomas G Stone,* hitting her propeller. She was forced to fall out of the convoy and was towed to Algiers. The landing went off without much opposition at any of the beaches and the *Strathnaver* entered Algiers Bay in the forenoon of 9 November. She was ordered alongside but no definite berth was allotted and Captain Coates decided, in conference with the pilot, that the best wharf available was the east side of the Mole *Louis Billiand.* A small French ship was moored head and stern about 150ft off the wharf and parallel to it. There was a fresh northeasterly wind blowing and as the *Strathnaver* approached the breakwater, unaided by tugs as there were none available, the first enemy planes came over and, although it was a comparatively mild raid, a heavy bomb fell a few hundred yards off her port quarter.

At 4pm a heavy attack developed and one of the warships received a direct hit which caused a fire aft. The RAF made their first appearance in this raid and 11 enemy aircraft were shot down. At dusk minelaying and torpedo aircraft were active in the bay and out at sea, but no ships in the anchorage

'Operation Torch' and the follow-up convoys were extremely costly for the P&O Company. Their most prestigious ship, the *Strathallan*, was the last of the company's vessels lost during the Second World War. Here she is seen burning fiercely and listing to port, with the salvage tug *Restive* alongside her. *(P&O)*

were damaged. During the next day there were air raids inland and at 2am on 11 November another raid took place, during which a heavy bomb fell about 200 yards away from the *Strathnaver*. She sailed from Algiers at 8pm that day with the 36th Infantry Brigade Group on board and set course for Bougie to the east. She arrived off the port at 6.45am on 12 November and ran right into a torpedo-bombing and minelaying attack, during which a torpedo passed close astern of the ship. The aircraft flew close to the water and they seemed to be no more than a ship's length away. At the same time a heavy bombing raid developed on the ships in the anchorage and as they approached the port they saw the P&O liner *Cathay* burning fiercely. A signal was received saying that magnetic mines had been laid in the approaches to the harbour, so Captain Coates anchored well clear. A corvette came alongside and took off the majority of the troops, then the remainder disembarked in the ship's landing-craft. At 9.30am, with disembarkation completed, Captain Coates requested that minesweepers escort him into the harbour and two of these ships did so. As the *Strathnaver* approached the harbour, an attack was made by six aircraft and a stick of bombs just missed the blazing wreck of the *Cathay*. More bombs fell close to the craft which had disembarked the *Strathnaver's* troops and incendiaries fell close to the *Strathnaver's* starboard bow. The ship's AA gunners were firing continuously at the enemy aircraft while the ship was

manoeuvering and making fast in the harbour. Very little of their ammunition was wasted firing at aircraft which were out of range and there was some good shooting, with several hits observed. Captain Coates berthed the ship close to a high, steep hill and there is no doubt that this afforded the ship some protection as it prevented aircraft from getting a clear run in over her. At 1.30pm there was an attack by seven aircraft and at 3pm a formation of ten enemy aircraft was spotted coming in over the hill which was on the *Strathnaver's* starboard side and it was clear the attack was directed at her. Several heavy bombs fell on shore near to the ship and two fell in the sea some 20 yards off her starboard quarter. The explosion from these brought down some of the pipe-lagging in the engine-room. Captain Coates was convinced that this raid was broken up by the prompt and accurate fire of his bofors and other guns' crews. Control of the Oerlikans was carried out by loud hailer with great success and in the words of his report: 'As it was essential that the work of the ship should go on, even during air raids, the "air alarm" was not sounded but, as orders were always broadcast for guns' crews to close up throughout the ship, warning was passed to all that a raid was imminent. The breaks between raids were few and short. Throughout the practically continuous raids at Bougie the behaviour of the crew, in all departments, was excellent. For example, while entering the harbour, current was cut off the winches in order to minimize the risk of fire

The *Strathnaver* in Aden Harbour, 16 March 1962, on her way to the breaker's yard at Hong Kong, where she arrived on 1 April 1962. Ten months later, in February 1963, the author saw her alongside a quay at Ngautaukok and breaking up had only just begun in earnest. *(Duncan Smedley)*

The *Stratheden* alongside her berth at Pyrmont, Sydney on a fine, sunny day in the early 1960s. *(Don Smith)*

An aerial view of the *Strathallan* on fire, with her funnel buckled by the heat. The *Restive* lies aft on her port side. *(G. Milne)*

and, although a raid was in progress, the Lascars carried on hoisting the three-ton derricks by hand. During the attacks 3,204 rounds of Oerlikan and 216 rounds of bofors ammunition were expended, as well as 853 rounds of other types of ammunition and 82 rockets. Most of the bombers were JU88s and the torpedo bombers were Italian S79s.'

At 10pm on 12 November *Strathnaver* cleared Bougie and sailed for Algiers, and apart from some attention from an enemy reconnaissance aircraft, which dropped a flare close to the ship, no more air activity was encountered.

Meanwhile on the Clyde preparations were under way for large follow-up convoys of troop transports to leave for North Africa, which now involved the other four *Strath* liners. On the same day that the *Strathnaver* left Bougie, the *Stratheden* left Loch na Keal for the Clyde and there she joined the *Strathaird*, which had just completed a long refit during which her boilers were partially retubed. Also there were the *Strathmore*, which had suffered serious engine trouble earlier that year and the *Strathallan*. In the words of Captain Baillie of the *Stratheden:* 'It was obvious that we were on the very eve of embarkation. An enormous fleet of grey-painted transports filled even that wide expanse of water; every large shipping company in Britain was represented, and under their wartime disguise many of the famous pre-war passenger liners could be observed.' The second troop convoy left the Clyde on 14 November 1942 and six days later, at 1am, they passed Gibraltar. Mr George Milne, who was on the *Strathallan*, recalls spending two days at Algiers before intense bombing raids forced an early departure: 'At Algiers on the 22nd, 23rd and 24th November bombers arrived every half-hour and

maybe it was just more by good luck that there were more misses than direct hits. The AA guns kept up a terrific barrage of fire-power which contributed to make things difficult for the enemy. With the noise and action sleep was difficult and it caused quite an inconvenience. The engine-room Pakistanis never seemed particularly concerned, they would just say, "Germans Bobri wallahs" meaning "Germans cause a lot of trouble".' She steamed back to Glasgow via Gibraltar, and she arrived home again on 2 December 1942.

The *Strathallan* left the Clyde, once again bound for Algiers on 11 December 1942, commanded by Captain John Henry Biggs who was, according to Commodore John Wacher, then a cadet on board the *Strathallan*, a most charming and well-loved man. As well as her crew of 466, there were 296 military officers, 248 nurses and 4,112 troops. Amongst these were the headquarters staff of the American First Army, which included Kay Sumersbee, General Eisenhower's private secretary, and Helen Bourke-White, the intrepid reporter from *Life* magazine. The *Strathallan* was commodore ship in what was designated convoy KMF5, under the command of Commodore Dennison. Unknown to anyone in the convoy, in mid-November that year a 'most secret' signal to the Admiralty from Gibraltar had warned of strong concentrations of U-boats on either side of the Straits, waters through which the 'Torch' convoys had to pass. It warned that: 'The most effective measures of which we are capable will be necessary if we are to avoid crippling losses in troop transports.' To counter this threat the USAF made as many air raids as possible on the U-boat bases in France, and all merchant ships over 10,000 tons were ordered to zigzag at all times, except in heavy weather. The voyage down the Atlantic was without incident, apart from severe weather conditions which damaged some ships and caused condenser problems in the *Strathallan* forcing her to a standstill for half an hour on 16 December. With hostile aircraft having been reported only a few hours earlier this caused some concern at the Admiralty and the destroyer *Lightning* was ordered to stand by her. Fortunately she was soon back with the convoy and the following day, with the severe weather abating, the convoy was able to increase speed.

The convoy passed safely through the Straits of Gibraltar and in the early hours of 21 December the Oran section of the convoy detached just north of the port. At 2.25am that morning on a smooth sea and with good visibility under a full moon, the *Strathallan* was steaming at 14 knots on a course of 94° in a position close to the end of the Oran swept channel, when she crossed the path of U562, commanded by Lieutenant Horst Hamm, which had managed to break through the escort screen. One torpedo fired by the U-boat struck the *Strathallan* on the port side in the engine-room. The explosion was very loud and according to Captain Biggs: 'The force of it shook the whole ship and a couple of tables in my cabin were broken.' George Milne recalls: 'I was sound asleep when it happened. The explosion seemed to cause a vacuum in the cabin making breathing difficult for about five seconds.' Sadly all the staff on duty in the engine-room were killed instantly; they were Mr Norman Knox, a Junior Engineer, Mr H. S. Morley, the Third Engineer, and two Asian crew members.

The violence of the explosion threw a huge column of water over the ship and No 8 boat was blown over the head of the davits, where it landed upside-down and could not be dislodged. There was a large hole in the liner's port side, damage was caused to the bulkhead between the engine-and boiler-rooms and also to the port after settling tanks, which caused oil fuel to leak out into the boiler-room, and it was this oil which was to determine the ship's fate. All lights and power failed and the vessel immediately took on a 15° list to port, which was later corrected by counterflooding. In the boiler-room, which was directly forward of the engine-room, Mr J. Simpson, the Supernumerary Fourth Engineer on duty, was lifted two feet off the plates and dropped. Despite being shocked he got all his staff out of the boiler-room and shut down the boiler fires. The emergency diesel generator was started, emergency lighting throughout the ship was switched on, power was put on to the steering-gear and the emergency pumps were put on to the engine-and boiler-rooms.

The story is now best told by Captain Biggs who wrote his report for the Ministry of Transport on 8 January 1943. He stated that: 'Boat Stations was sounded on the alarm gongs. We carried four motor boats, 16 lifeboats all fitted with Fleming Gear (hand propelling apparatus), which held roughly 1,600 and enough rafts to take the remainder with some to spare. In fine weather we keep a number of lifeboats swung out and lowered to each deck, so that they are always ready for an emergency. Troops and crew were mustered quickly by means of megaphones and messengers, and boats were manned. Everybody remained very steady and behaved extremely well, but several men (troops) did jump overboard. The sea being smooth and the possibilty of being hit again

by a second or third torpedo being probable, I gave orders to lower the boats. They all got away except the damaged No 8 boat and No 9b boat, which it was found impossible to launch owing to the list of the ship. We did try to push this boat out with the assistance of 80 to 100 troops, but found it impossible to move it. I learned later that No's 12 and 14 boats were found to have a lot of water in them which was probably thrown up by the explosion and No 14 boat became waterlogged, being probably holed. The rafts were then cleared away and some were launched with their painters fast on board in readiness. The list of the ship at this time was 10°, but it gradually increased to 12° as the water gained in the engine-room. The Chief Engineer, Mr G.J. MacLennon, reported that the after engine-room bulkhead was intact and the carpenter reported that all the compartments except the engine-room and boiler-room were nearly dry. All remaining troops were ordered to keep to the starboard side of the vessel to ease the list.'

Mr Charles Lowe of Bournemouth, who had joined the Orient Line as a musician and who, on the outbreak of war, became a steward, was in the forepeak mess, nicknamed the 'gloryhole', at the forward end of E Deck. He remembers the torpedoing of the ship clearly: 'Sunday 20 December 1942 had been a hard day and, being very tired, I turned in at 10.30pm. I was in a deep sleep when the torpedo struck the ship and, for just a few seconds, I thought that we had collided. Apart from the emergency dynamo there were no lights, and the peak was in uproar with most of the occupants gone before I had even donned my pullover. One of my chums went without even saying a word and I asked another friend, Phil Elwis, whether he was going to take his clarinet. I made sure that mine was fixed firmly to my haversack straps and then made a very short visit to the toilet nearby. When I got back to the peak there was only one occupant left and, having stuffed handkerchiefs and my wallet into my pockets and with my haversack on my back, I left for the upper deck. I can remember wondering whether I would ever see the peak again. I was fully clothed with my tweed jacket and mackintosh on, and with the ship listing about 10° to port it was not easy to climb the companion-ways.

Once out on deck I found that it was a beautifully clear night, with a bright, full moon. However, on deck there was pandemonium with soldiers shouting and tearing about all over the place. Boats were already being lowered and, as I crewed a boat, I had to hurry over to it. When I got there I found that it had already been lowered to just below C Deck and I had to climb down to it, before we were lowered quickly to the water. The motor started easily and as we drew away from the *Strathallan* we were able to pick up a few people from the sea.

Commodore John F. Wacher CBE RD RNR, who was a cadet aboard the *Strathallan*, recalls the ship's boats being launched: 'While the boats were being launched and as many nurses and troops were getting away as fast as possible, I remember a voice over a loud hailer in the darkness saying, "*Strathallan*, are you all right?" It was the commanding officer of a destroyer which had come back to stand by us and this destroyer subsequently took the *Strathallan* in tow. Whilst this was going on the boats were being lowered and filled to well over capacity, because in wartime this had to be done. An interesting and unexpected difficulty was that some men "froze" on the long embarkation ladders and would neither move up nor down for some time, because of a normal fear of heights. Unfortunately some over enthusiastic people had started to throw the old-fashioned heavy wooden life-rafts overboard with the intention of picking up others left on board. The ropes attached to these became tangled in the propellers in Cadet H.R. Wade's and my lifeboat. We just had to jump overboard and cut the rope away. I was, in fact, aided by Mr Simpson, the Fourth Engineer, who, unbeknown to me, had already been deeply shocked in the boiler-room when the torpedo struck. Without hesitation he jumped over and helped me clear the ropes which took some 20 or 30 minutes. We were then unceremoniously hauled back on board and managed to pull clear of the ship. Shortly afterwards a destroyer came to the area and told us that we would be picked up in the morning. As I recall it, as a cadet of 17½ years, it was not too bad in my boat as there were 88 nurses and I spent quite a lot of the night being sick into their tin hats.'

Patrick Miles, who was Supernumerary Second Officer recalls: 'I was fast asleep in my bunk at the time and woke up having felt a bump. I had left my light on when I fell asleep and at that moment it, and all the lights in the ship, failed. I hurriedly dressed and felt my way from the officers' quarters to my boat station, supervising the port side of the Boat Deck. Luckily it was a clear night and there was sufficient light to see by, and I noticed that there were two lifeboats which had been unseated by the explosion and were inoperable. Shortly afterwards the first of the crew and troops arrived to take up their proper station, and I noticed the purser with the ship's papers, boarding the motor boat. The order to abandon ship had already been given, so embarking the boats proceeded in an orderly manner. It was some time before I realized that all the women, the QAs and correspondents, were stationed two decks below and had been temporarily forgotten. This was rectified and they started filing up two decks to the lifeboats.'

From his lifeboat Charles Lowe looked back to the ship where, 'I could see that it still seemed to be a scene of absolute uproar, and I could see some nurses who were screaming and hanging on to rope ladders. Watching the nurses still on board the ship made me, sitting comfortably in the boat, feel quite guilty. Rafts were being flung blindly over the side and they must have fallen on or very close to swimmers in the water. A raft with two people clinging to it went by and we dragged them on board the boat to find that they were two of my chums.

Suddenly the propeller of our boat seized up and we began to drift some distance from the ship. However, a cadet in our boat got undressed and dived over the side to free it and we were then able to start the engine. About two hours later we were ordered to return to the ship, which we did and, once alongside, I decided to climb up the scrambling net and back on to the *Strathallan*.'

At 4am, with all the bulkheads still intact, and with the emergency pumps holding their own, the destroyer HMS *Laforey* came to take the *Strathallan* in tow but, owing to the limited amount of power on the capstains, it was two hours before towing commenced. At 6.30am things looked hopeful as the emergency bilge-pumps were reported to be gaining on the water in the stokehold. George Milne, together with an engineer, Bill Meson, tended the emergency diesel generator that forenoon and he recalls: 'We got hold of a bucket and heating element and took tea and biscuits on a tray to Captain Biggs on the bridge. I always remember his remark, "Good God, where did this come from?" But it was most acceptable.'

Once back on deck Charles Lowe remembers: 'There were still plenty of troops on board and I went forward to where I saw some of the ship's company out on deck, and we all helped to haul ropes up from a destroyer which was going to take us in tow. However, they were far too heavy and we found it impossible without a winch and I went off to try and clean the thick grease from my hands. I was then told that I would be helping to serve a meal at 8am and so I went down to the galley. It was very eerie inside the ship with very little light and the water gently lapping up the companion-ways one deck below. Once into the galley I started to make sandwiches of corned beef with lots of butter. After this I walked round the accommodation on my own and as it was so silent it gave me quite a peculiar feeling. At 9am I turned in hoping to get a bit of sleep, but I was shaken at 10am and told that the boilers might go up at any minute.'

At 10.20am over 1,000 of the remaining troops were taken off by a destroyer and Captain Biggs suggested to the escorting destroyers that the remainder, numbering about 3,000, be disembarked. The troops were in good spirits having had a makeshift meal of bread and herrings, and were passing the time with community singing to a piano on the upper decks. Sergeant L. A. Friend remembers going below that morning to collect his personal belongings, to find his bedding floating around in murky water. At 1pm that day, Captain Biggs felt optimistic that his ship would manage to get into Oran, but the emergency bilge-pumps were failing and Captain Biggs could see the discharge overboard getting less and less. The salvage tug *Restive* came alongside to assist with the pumping. However, at 1.15pm, as the water level in the boiler-room continued to rise, with the oil which was leaking from the port after settling-tanks floating on the surface, it came into contact with the still very hot brickwork in the boilers and in the words of Captain Biggs: 'There was a terrific noise as the gas exploded, flames shot high out of the funnel and continued burning fiercely, the paint on the funnel and ventilators burning and dropping off.' Just before the explosion the destroyer HMS *Pathfinder* had taken off further troops, leaving just 1,000 on board. Returning to Captain Biggs' report, he explains what happened next: 'Going below I examined the bulkheads in B, C, D and E Decks and found them already red-hot with paint and woodwork smouldering. I found that H Deck was under water and G Deck half under water. The remaining six decks were catching fire very quickly. It seemed hopeless, but I ordered the emergency fire-pumps to be started and fire-hoses were passed up from the tug *Restive*. The ammunition from the magazine on A Deck was thrown overboard. This was done quickly, but the fire could not be tackled in so many places, and the whole centre of the ship was soon ablaze. I returned to the bridge through dense smoke, and almost immediately flames shot up through the B Deck lounge to the officers' quarters. Cadet McKibben, who was at the wheel, remained there until ordered away by me, and we both had to drop over the fore side of the bridge and run through smoke to amidships on C Deck where the tug was alongside. I then went aft and ordered "abandon ship".'

Charles Lowe recalls that he, '...spent the morning on the forecastle watching the destroyer tow us and as it was such a gloriously hot day I stripped off to the waist. At about 11.30am one of the destroyers, which was packed with the lifeboat survivors, went speeding by. Then, at just after midday there was a huge roar as flames came shooting out of the *Strathallan's* funnel. The heat was intense and the noise deafening, so I got dressed again and took myself off to the pantry where I made some jam sandwiches. When I went back on deck the last of the army officers were being embarked into a large tug or destroyer aft. Soon after this I was told to muster on C Deck aft, but before I could go I had to help with a fire-hose. However, this made little difference to the flames and, with the fires getting rapidly worse, I had to run aft with my bag. After throwing my case down first, I climbed down the scrambling net and on to the tug. Looking back I saw Captain Biggs and the Chief Engineer scrambling down the net with flames licking round them.'

Patrick Miles remembers leaving the ship thus: 'In the early afternoon it was noticed that the funnel paint was flaking off, due to the fact that the water in the bottom of the ship, covered with fuel oil, had risen to the level of the still hot furnaces, which immediately created a fierce fire which rose from the bottom of the ship. Every effort was made to quench the fire with the very limited water from the emergency pumps. It was obvious that nothing further could be done and in the late afternoon the order was given to abandon ship. I had been playing a hose on the fire in C Deck, in complete darkness except for the light from the fire and, on a shout from the Chief Officer, found my way to daylight and up to the Boat Deck to see if I could get to my cabin in order to collect valuables. The Boat Deck was already bursting into flames in various places and the officers' quarters had already been engulfed. I proceeded forward and joined the remainder on the starboard side of C Deck, waiting our turn to scramble down to the tug. This was not pleasant as the ship's side was already very hot and rivets were popping out like machine-gun bullets.'

Just before he left the ship, George Milne recalls going down to the generator compartment: 'I didn't stay long, it was eerie when all you could see were white lagged pipes disappearing into the oil and seawater.' He also remembers the Chief Engineer abandoning ship with his canary under his uniform cap and also the ship's cat under his arm. At about 2pm the *Laforey* ceased the tow and everyone transferred to her from the *Restive*, which then took up towing the stricken *Strathallan*. George Milne remembers that they circled round the ship, which was burning furiously, and as each coat of paint burnt off, '...the ship amazingly began turning to her peacetime colours. The funnel buckled and fell backwards.'

Forty members of the *Laforey's* crew went on board the after end of the *Strathallan* to dump the 6-inch ammunition and to investigate the possibility of doing more to save the ship, but they were soon recalled. Towing continued until 4am on 22 December, when the *Strathallan*, the newest of the five 'White Sisters' rolled over onto her port side and sank. The position was 36°-01'N/00°-33'W, about 12 miles from Oran.

There were many brave acts in the tireless efforts to save this fine ship. Captain Biggs was awarded the CBE, Mr G.J. MacLennon, the Chief Engineer and Mr J.C.W. Last, the Chief Officer, the OBE. Mr J. Simpson, the Fourth Engineer, the MBE. Six members of the crew, including Cadet T.R. St C. McKibben, were awarded the BEM and four crew members, including Cadets Wade and Wacher received Commendations.

The successful 'Torch' landings served as a preliminary to the landings in Italy and Normandy, but the P&O Company suffered heavily. Five large ships, totalling some 85,980 gross tons, and including the *Viceroy of India* and the *Strathallan*, were lost.

Most of the *Strathallan's* crew returned to the UK in the Canadian Pacific liner *Duchess of Richmond*, which had also been part of the same convoy.

Chapter Eleven

Peace At Last

By mid-May 1943 all the Axis forces in North Africa had surrendered and the next major Allied effort was to be directed at Italy. Once again the *Strath* liners were to be represented in the campaign, this time by the *Strathnaver*. She had in fact been fitted out as what was called at the time, 'landing ship infantry', and the main feature of the conversion was the replacement of the ship's lifeboats with assault landing-craft. In April 1943 the *Strathnaver* anchored in Suez Bay, off Port Tewfik, and stayed there for over a month whilst her landing-craft crews and troops trained for the intended landings. On a number of occasions the troop transports, which also included HMS *Keren* (ex BISN *Kenya*) and the Orient liner SS *Otranto,* put to sea in order to practise the manoeuvres which would have to be carried out in the dark and without signals. Mr A.E. Piper, who was serving aboard the *Strathnaver* remembers: 'Eventually we were told of the invasion and that we could have anything of value, including a will, put ashore for safe keeping.' On 10 June 1943 the squadron embarked the assault troops, 7,000 men of the Hampshire and the Devon & Dorset Regiments, and steamed down the Red Sea and up the Gulf of Aqaba where they anchored close inshore. The beach at the head of the Gulf had been prepared and a full-scale dress rehearsal was carried out. The squadron, which had been code-named 'Group N', returned to Suez and on 5 July that year they left Port Said to carry out 'Operation Husky', the object of which was to invade and capture the south-east part of Sicily.

The convoy skirted the coast of North Africa until just east of Malta when it altered course for the Sicilian coast. On the afternoon of 9 July, fleet minesweepers and LCIs joined the convoy, and at 1am the next morning, having arrived at the release position, the landing-craft were loaded with troops and lowered. The ships were about seven miles from the coast, and at 1.15am the flotilla of landing-craft left for the shore.

At exactly 2.45am the whole shoreline appeared to be lit up by gunfire and the pre-arranged Very lights informed the ships that the beaches had been captured. Fortunately there had been little opposition and the three troop transports were able to anchor close to Marzamemi Beach where the landings were completed.

By 11 July 1943, despite some resistance, the Allied forces had fanned out from the beach-heads and British and US troops linked up the next day at Ragusa. They had captured six airfields and the US 1st Infantry Division had hurled back a German counter-attack which had been spearheaded by 100 tanks. The *Strathnaver* stayed off Sicily long enough to embark the wounded before departing for Malta. After this she steamed home through the Mediterranean in convoy, before returning once again to the campaign in Italy where she followed the Allied forces up Italy as they advanced northwards.

In August 1943 the *Strathnaver* left Liverpool for a trooping voyage to New York, but she had to put in to St John's, Newfoundland, with engine and boiler problems. Once they were repaired she put to sea, but whilst leaving the port she struck an uncharted rock in the harbour entrance and she had to return once again to the dockyard at St John's for repairs and she did not get to New York until October that year.

Meanwhile, her sister ship *Strathaird* left the Clyde on 25 February 1943 for a nine-month voyage, most of which was spent in the Indian Ocean carrying troops between South Africa, Suez, Aden and India. On her return voyage to the Clyde in October that year she called at Pointe Noire in the Belgian Congo, an unusual port for P&O ships.

Archie Allan of Glasgow was a gunner aboard the *Strathaird* in the spring of 1944 and he recalls the ship lying in the King George V Dock at Shieldhall, off the Renfrew

The *Strathnaver* at Algiers in early 1945, just before the end of the war in Europe.
(Captain R.N. Firth)

The first of the 'White Sisters' to return to her peacetime role was the *Stratheden*.

(*F.R. Sherlock*)

Road in Glasgow: 'We duly disembarked our troops and passengers, and the cargo was unloaded. The cleaners then came aboard and cleaned everything in readiness for our next complement. We did what were called sabotage watches, mainly to watch the radar tower. During this time the great buildup to the Normandy invasion was reaching its climax and there was a lot of speculation as to where we were going next. Soon the troops started embarking along with the usual sprinkling of civilians and it soon became clear that we were going east again, as the troops were all carrying tropical gear.' The *Strathaird* sailed on 29 March 1944 and Archie Allan takes up the story once again: 'We went downstream to the Tail of the Bank and joined the rest of the convoy and I must say it was a lot better than my first trip, with the weather fine and everyone feeling that the tide was turning for us. The days went quickly, with boat drills and practice shoots, and soon we were going through the Straits of Gibraltar again, with only one or two action station calls. We went straight through the Med with only a few alarms at the danger spots after Malta. Then it was Port Said, through the Canal to Port Tewfik, where we had a break and held boat races between the gun crews and ship's company, which the troops and passengers enjoyed. Through the Red Sea the black-out was relaxed and our next stop was Aden then on to Bombay. Shortly before we arrived in the port there had been an enormous explosion in the docks, with many casualties. I heard that a ship's propeller was blown two miles inland and some of the fires were still smouldering.* We had to go into dry dock in Bombay for work on the ship's bearings, but the shore engineers soon had the *Strathaird* in good order and we were once again homeward bound. We soon got back into the sea-watches and the troops had to be familiarized with boat stations and drills. Soon it was Aden and the Red Sea again, then through the Canal to Port Said where, I'm sorry to say, my association with the *Strathaird* ended.'

The *Strathmore* sailed from Liverpool to the Clyde in late October 1944 and from there to Bombay. Mr G.L. Jones recalls: 'We experienced our first real air attack, between Gibraltar and Port Said. I believe it was on 6 November, at about 5pm. I was on duty in the boiler-room when we heard the AA guns firing and were warned of an attack on the convoy. It was a bit nerve-racking down below, as there was nothing we could do but wait. Fortunately we came through without damage, though I believe one ship was damaged. On the positive side, one aircraft was hit and part of the plane landed on the deck of the *Almanzora*, the ship directly ahead of us. We called at Port Said, Aden and Bombay, then returned to Liverpool having called at Port Augusta in Sicily, in the Italian war zone. From Liverpool we made a quick trip across the Atlantic to Boston and picked up US troops.' After this the *Strathmore* made five voyages between the UK and Bombay, and she was on one of these when the war in Europe ended. Mr Jones made his last passage in the *Strathmore* when she left Liverpool in August 1945: 'We sailed from Liverpool to Gibraltar and Malta, then to Taranto in Italy to pick up and repatriate Australian and New Zealand ex-POWs. We called at Colombo before heading for Melbourne, Wellington and Burnie in Tasmania. The quayside reception

*Two enormous explosions on 14 April 1944, in the docks area of Bombay, killed as many as 940 people. The freighter *Fort Stikine*, carrying 1,300 tons of TNT, caught fire. As water was poured on the ship to contain the blaze, the munitions exploded. Another larger explosion occurred minutes later, obliterating the *Fort Stikine* and 19 other ships. Millions of pounds worth of damage was done and 40,000 tons of food were lost, leading to semi-famine conditions in India.

at those ports will never be forgotten, with military bands and crowds on the dockside, quite a contrast to our arrival in Southampton where we were met by a few "brass hats" and one or two VIPs. In all the *Strathmore* was a lucky and happy ship throughout the war, with both discipline and morale very good. Two things we had to be wary of were, (a) as engineers, not to make black smoke when at sea and (b) to make sure we were never in the barber's chair when the 6-inch gun, mounted on the deck just above the shop, was fired, especially if the barber was holding a razor.'

The end of the war in Europe saw the other three *Straths* carrying troops to India, where there was a need for reinforcements for the campaign against the Japanese. By 6 May 1945, although fighting continued in some sectors, the campaign in Burma was declared over and plans were in hand for the invasion of Malaya and the reoccupation of Singapore. Fortunately, on 2 September 1945, Japan formally surrendered after the atomic bombs were dropped on Hiroshima and Nagasaki, and the Second World War was over. For the four remaining 'White Sisters' the additional hazards at sea were over, but they would remain in their role of troop transports for the first few months of peace.

Tilbury Docks 1945. Although the war is over and *Strathaird's* 6-inch gun is being removed, she still had another year's service as a troop transport before being handed back to P&O.

(Captain R.N. Firth)

Chapter Twelve

The Return To Trade

When the Second World War ended, Britain, although victorious, was virtually bankrupt. For six years the country had poured its vast industrial capacity and wealth totally into the war effort and there would be as many problems recovering from victory as Germany would face recovering from defeat. The British Mercantile Marine was now some 30 per cent smaller than it had been at the beginning of the war, yet to survive Britain had to export far more than she had in pre-war days. Vast armies had been raised both in Britain and in the Commonwealth countries and these troops had to be repatriated, and only Britain had the troopship capacity available for this enormous task. There were also Britain's world-wide commitments to her Empire, which were complicated by the rise of nationalism, particularly in the East, and by communist agitation which would require large numbers of troops for internal security duties. So it was inevitable that the 'White Sisters' would continue in their role of troop transports, with their cargo capacity now taken up with exporting and importing goods, instead of war materials.

The *Stratheden*, being the most modern of P&O's liners, was the first ship to be released by the government, although she spent ten months on trooping duties before this. In July 1945 she was the first troopship to enter the St Lawrence River for Quebec, and her large complement of returning Canadian troops received an enthusiastic reception. In October 1945 she left Liverpool carrying over 2,000 members of the RAAF and 1,800 New Zealand servicemen back to their home countries. On the return voyage she embarked over 6,000 servicemen and women from Singapore and India and returned them home to Southampton in early December. On her next voyage she again carried over 5,000 troops, together with some civilian ex-internees from the Far East. She made only one more trooping voyage to Bombay and back between May and July 1946, before leaving London for Barrow-in-Furness on 27 July for reconditioning at government expense for her normal peacetime trade. Originally she was to have been ready for service in the New Year of 1947, but there were severe problems in the shipbuilding industry, mainly due to long delays in the supply of skilled labour, and so it was June 1947 before she was ready to sail once again. By that time there was a waiting list of prospective passengers which ran into thousands and they were clamouring for berths. With austerity and rationing under the post-war Labour government in Britain even more severe than it had been during the war, many people had decided to emigrate to Australia and New Zealand. This was encouraged by the generous subsidies from the Australian government, and in the spring of 1947 the complaints about delays had become so numerous that P&O felt obliged to issue a statement explaining the problems in the shipyards.

The *Stratheden* left Tilbury in June 1947, commanded by Captain S.W.S. Dickson, and Captain D.G.O. Baillie recalls the occasion: 'The *Stratheden* was the first of our ships to have been converted back to her pre-war status and after nine years of ships stripped to the bare steel, it was an agreeable experience to board her at Tilbury Landing Stage, to find the clock put back to 1939. The rows of stewards in their spotless white jackets drawn up and waiting to take your hand luggage; the glistening white paint of the ship's superstructure towering above you and the long-forgotten atmosphere of solid luxury and willing service ready to engulf you as soon as you stepped over the gangway entrance platform and into the foyer.' As the ship steamed through the Mediterranean Sea he also recalls: 'Steaming close in to the North African coast in clear weather we could see Algiers distinctly; it was curious to think that when the *Stratheden* and I had last been together in those waters she had looked very different in her grey paint, her superstructure bristling with guns and life-rafts, as she bore towards the shore 5,000 troops waiting in some tension to land, instead of 1,000 passengers who now leaned over the rails admiring the view in hot sunshine.'

Len Wyeth, who was the Senior Assistant Purser on board, remembers that one of his jobs was to teach the new Women Assistant Pursers, who had been appointed to the sea staff. He also remembers the thousands of visitors who swarmed over the ship in Australian ports and, '...relentlessly helped themselves to the ship's writing paper, envelopes and everything with the ship's name on it. The crowds on board were so dense that it was impossible to move in the alleyways.' He also remembers that he had to explain to head office the reason for one and a half tons of stationery being used whilst off the Australian ports.

The *Strathaird* made three more voyages as a troop transport after the end of the war. The first two took her to Bombay and during the second voyage she called at Mombasa and Karachi as well as Piraeus and Salonika. The third voyage took her to Singapore, calling at Port Swettenham and Madras and arriving back in London on 20 August 1946. One month later, on 21 September, she left Tilbury for Newcastle upon Tyne, where she arrived the next day and was handed over to Vickers Armstrong for reconditioning. During the war she had steamed 387,745 miles and had carried 128,961 personnel. Like the *Stratheden* her refit was prolonged by the acute shortages, and instead of taking six months as scheduled, the work lasted over a year. During the reconditioning the two dummy funnels were removed, which gave more deck space for the first class passengers. She left Walker on Tyne on 20 December 1947, 15 months after her arrival, and finally sailed from an austere and frozen Britain for Australia on 22 January 1948. She was commanded by Captain H.S. Allen RD RNR who, during war service in the Royal Navy, had received a Mention in Despatches.

The *Strathmore* too made voyages to India and the Far East following the end of the war, and on 15 November 1945 she arrived at Southampton from Bombay with over 3,000 men from the 2nd Army Division and other units. On her next voyage, in March 1946, she transported Japanese prisoners from Bombay and Singapore to Kure in Japan. During 1946 and 1947, as well as the more familiar ports, she called at

22 September 1946 and the *Strathaird* arrives on the Tyne for her post-war refit and refurbishment. *(Author's Collection)*

Following the end of the war the *Strathmore* made trooping voyages to India and the Far East. In this view, which was taken on 15 February 1946, she is entering Malta's Grand Harbour on a voyage to the Far East. *(M. Cassar)*

The *Strathnaver* was the last of the 'White Sisters' to be handed back to P&O. She remained on government service for over three years after the war ended. This photograph, taken on 17 July 1947, shows her arriving at Southampton.

(Southampton City Museums)

STRATHNAVER 15·5·48

On 15 May 1948, three years after the end of the war in Europe, the *Strathnaver* was still on government service as a troopship. Here she is seen leaving Malta.

(M. Cassar)

The *Strathnaver* was reconditioned for service as a passenger liner at the end of 1948, and during the refit her two dummy funnels were removed. This view shows the first class Sports Deck after the work had been carried out. (P&O)

Shanghai, Hong Kong and Singapore on trooping duties. It was early May 1948 before she completed her last voyage on government service and she lay at Tilbury Docks with the *Strathaird,* which now had only one funnel, and the *Strathnaver,* which still had the original three. On June 14 1948 the *Strathmore* left Tilbury for Newcastle upon Tyne where she also underwent a refit by Vickers Armstrong, which was completed on 8 October, four months later. It was 27 October 1948 before she too left Tilbury for her first post-war voyage to Bombay and Sydney.

The last of the four sisters to be returned to the P&O Company was the *Strathnaver* and she remained on government service for over three years after the war ended. Still fitted out as a troop transport, she was employed on voyages to India and Australia and also to the Far East, where she called at Kure after carrying Japanese POWs from Singapore back to their homeland. They were put into the 'tween deck accommodation which was fitted out with three-tiered bunks and which was exceptionally clean. It was a far cry from the squalid conditions which the Japanese had imposed on the Allied POWs when they were being sent to Japan in the war years. Captain E. Mortleman-Lewis of Ringwood remembers that the Japanese POWs were very well-behaved and gave no trouble at all. He also recalls that on one stay in Kure he was able to visit Hiroshima, to see the devastation of that once beautiful city. During her voyages in the Far East she called at a number of unlikely ports including Shanghai and Woosung.

In October 1946 the *Strathnaver* collided with the 900-ton cargo ship *Fluor* at Southampton Docks. The liner had called at the port on her return from Bombay and was leaving for Tilbury when the mishap occurred as she was swinging off a berth adjoining the *Fluor's.* The *Strathnaver's* bows holed the smaller vessel amidships and she sank in eight minutes, but fortunately her 12-man crew were able to get ashore. The *Strathnaver* was undamaged and so was able to continue her voyage down Southampton Water. In May 1948 the *Strathnaver* and her sister *Strathaird* lay at Tilbury Docks together, the former ship on government service and with her three funnels, while the latter vessel was back in peacetime

service and with her single funnel. It was November 1948 before the *Strathnaver* completed her last voyage as a troopship, after nearly nine years of government service. During that time she had carried 129,000 troops and steamed 352,000 miles. On 2 November 1948 she left London for Belfast where, upon her arrival three days later, she was to be reconditioned for service as a passenger liner once again. The work took a year and during the refit her two dummy funnels were removed, bringing her appearance into line with that of her sister ship. It was 6 December 1949 before she left Belfast for London and 5 January 1950 before she made her first post-war voyage to Australia on the company's account, over ten years from the date when she had been requisitioned.

Although Captain Baillie was pleased to, 'find the clock put back to 1939' on the newly refitted *Stratheden,* there could be no going back for Britain's post-war trade. In August 1947 India was granted independence and split into the states of India and Pakistan. P&O's very existence had depended for 105 years on its trade with India and it was clear that with no soldiers and civil servants travelling between London and Bombay there would be a significant loss of trade to the company. The new countries were now forming their own mercantile marine fleets, so it was obvious that there would also be a loss of trade on the P&O cargo service. To add to these difficulties, the government mail contracts were never renewed, which meant the loss of an important subsidy and consequently a decline in the importance of the traditional overland route via Marseilles. Only homeward-bound ships would continue to use the port, but it was still convenient for those passengers who wished to avoid the Bay of Biscay. For P&O it meant that the company had to compete without the advantages of Empire.

With the increased building costs and with the change in trade patterns, the post-war building programme would not be as ambitious as that which had followed the First World War, and only two new large passenger liners were completed. They were the 28,000-ton *Himalaya,* for the Australian service, and the 24,000-ton *Chusan,* for the service to the Far East. The four *Straths* were now between 12 and 19 years old, and they were no longer the company's 'crack' ships.

The newly refurbished *Strathmore* looking resplendent in her white livery.

(*Author's Collection*)

Chapter Thirteen

The 1950s

One sign of the return to normality after the war was the resumption of the series of cricket test matches between England and Australia, and in March 1948 on the return leg of her first post-war voyage for the company the *Strathaird* carried Don Bradman's Australian test team. As well as Don Bradman himself the team included Ray Lindwall, the fast bowler. The ship left Sydney on 10 March 1948 and arrived in Tilbury on 16 April, five weeks later. Although this may seem a long time for the voyage, in the late 1940s it was the only way for the vast majority of travellers to make the journey. Heathrow was still a sea of mud as it was slowly being transformed into London's civil airport and the main terminal services were housed in marquees. BOAC's fleet was made up largely of ex-wartime military aircraft, one of which for example, the *Halifax* bomber, became the *Halton* with a capacity for ten passengers. Another, the *Lancaster* bomber, became BOAC's *Lancastrian* which carried 14 passengers. In 1946 one of these aircraft flew the 12,000 miles between Sydney and London in 63½ hours. It was obvious that it would be a long time before air transport replaced the passenger liner.

Mrs Anita Weston of Sydney, who was one of the new Women Assistant Pursers on board the *Strathmore*, remembers the vessel's first voyage after war service: 'I was sent to Newcastle to join the *Strathmore* after the refit and trials were held in the North Sea *en route* to Tilbury. On the return voyage Arthur Askey, his wife and daughter Anthea were amongst the passengers. For the fancy dress party he borrowed my winter uniform, but unfortunately I did not take a photograph.' Mr James Buy, who was a Purser in the *Stratheden* in mid-1950, recalls Arthur Askey travelling in that ship and delighting both first and tourist class passengers by putting on a show for them. In 1950 the *Stratheden* undertook an unusual duty when she augmented the Cunard service between Southampton and New York, being chartered by Cunard for four round voyages starting on 7 June that year. The charter was arranged in January 1950 with a minimum first class transatlantic fare of £107, which compared favourably with £116 on the *Mauretania*. The minimum tourist class fare was set at £57, which was the same rate as that quoted for the *Mauretania*. On her return to Tilbury from Sydney on 20 May that year, the *Stratheden* disembarked her passengers and went into dock for maintenance before taking on stores and proceeding to Southampton on 3 June to start her work for Cunard. Initially bookings for the four voyages had been good, but there were some cancellations at the last minute for, in June that year, the communist army of North Korea invaded the south of the country thereby triggering the Korean War. Anita Weston remembers how she was recruited for the charter voyages: 'Enquiries were made for staff who could speak foreign languages and I claimed eligibility as I could speak "American". (I was evacuated for five years during the war and was a graduate of Babylon High School, New York). The Superintendent Purser accepted my application and so I

joined for the four voyages from Southampton via Le Havre to New York, (on one voyage we also called at Halifax, NS). Amongst the additional staff on board was a Cunard Purser, Peter Dawes, as his supervision was essential for us to cope with the mountain of paperwork needed to be completed in the few days crossing the Atlantic.'

Although the P&O ships had called at US ports during the war, it was unusual to see them in peacetime and the arrival of the *Stratheden* on 13 June 1950 drew this headline from the *New York Herald Tribune*: 'British Liner Here With Odd Crew, Including Many Indian Moslems.' The article went on to highlight the very different weather conditions encountered by the *Stratheden* in the North Atlantic: 'A British luxury liner with a largely Oriental crew emerged from the fog-shrouded entrance to New York Harbor early yesterday morning and steamed virtually unobserved to a North River pier.' She had on board 450 passengers and she was berthed alongside Pier 90 at West Fiftieth Street at 8am that day. Captain Dickson had first visited New York in a sailing vessel in 1911 and his last visit had been in 1943, when he was master of the *Ile de France*. (In June 1940, when the French had capitulated, the vessel was at Singapore where she was taken over by the British authorities and became an Allied transport). The *Stratheden* made four voyages to New York and on the third trip called at Halifax, NS, as well. She made her last transatlantic departure from Southampton on 26 August 1950 and on her return leg she came back to London, instead of Southampton, in readiness to resume her place on the Indian and Australian service.

On Monday 20 February 1950, as the *Strathaird* was homeward bound from Sydney, and as she was proceeding slowly to her mooring in Colombo Harbour, a faulty electrical contact prevented the engineers from putting her main propulsion motors astern and she collided with the port side of a cargo steamer, *Steel Age*. The stem of the *Strathaird* was badly damaged over a 20 foot section and the port side of the cargo ship was heavily indented, but after temporary repairs to both vessels they were able to continue their voyages. A subsequent Court of Inquiry found that neither vessel was to blame and the unexpected machinery defect had caused the accident.

Captain Barry Thompson of Auckland, New Zealand, recalls his appointment to the *Strathmore* in early 1951: 'On 22 May I was appointed as "Super Second" (Supernumerary Second Officer) of the *Strathmore* at 33 berth in Tilbury. This was the first passenger ship I was to sail in. I found it quite demanding, because I had not been accustomed to timekeeping, the maintenance of a schedule, in the way that was required of P&O passenger ships. It took me a little time to really accustom myself to the urgency of doing everything to a schedule. We left Tilbury on 7 June 1951 and the voyage out to Australia was generally uneventful. However, in Colombo we had one minor mishap. We were at anchor on 25 June when the Pakistani frigate, *Zulfiquar*,* collided with

*Ex-River Class Frigate HMS *Deveron*, built 1942

The *Strathnaver* in her post-war guise with only one funnel. The new look suited both her and her sister, *Strathaird*. (*P&O*)

A magnificent aerial view of the *Strathmore* in Sydney Harbour during the 1950s. (*Vickers PLC*)

The *Strathnaver* at Spithead when she was chartered by the government to take official guests to see the Coronation Naval Review on 15 June 1953.   *(Maritime Photo Library)*

the *Strathmore*. A small amount of damage was done to the shell plating at F Deck level, requiring temporary repair and so we didn't leave Colombo until the evening of 26 June, a day behind schedule.' The circumstances were very similar to those of the *Strathaird's* the previous year, only this time it was the P&O vessel which was berthed when the *Zulfiquar,* which had also suffered engine trouble, collided with the *Strathmore's* starboard side in the vicinity of the galley area. Temporary repairs were quickly made and the liner was able to continue her voyage the next day.

In those days the entertainment on the *Straths,* as well as on the other P&O vessels, was mainly organized by the passengers themselves and Purser Jim Buy remembers the times when, 'The Staff Captain (now called Deputy Captain) was in charge of entertainment and his staff consisted of two sports quartermasters, one for each class, and a four-piece band (commonly known as the "prickly heat quartet"). At the start of each voyage a sports committee was formed from volunteer passengers and this would consist of a chairman and committee members with recognized responsibilities. Usually there would be one set of sports competitions before Bombay and another after. It is hard to appreciate now that in those days it could take up to three weeks to finish a deck tennis competition, whereas on today's cruise ships competitions are arranged and completed in one day. Things were more leisurely then. Ships' officers did assist at the "Crossing the Line" ceremony, and

passengers who were from the entertainment world might also give performances. Film shows were projected in the lounge, the passengers sitting on sofas, armchairs, or on additional seating which would be brought in. The lounge, of course, was not air-conditioned and there were some very hot film shows. Very often half the audience left during the show.' Another problem in those days before air-conditioning is recalled by Jim Buy: 'Since cabin doors were seldom closed in hot weather, curtains being drawn across to help air circulation, no individual cabin keys were supplied. Cabin stewards would each have a key for their section and in port, when cabin stewards were off, key stewards were on duty, one on each deck. An additional hazard for passengers wishing to proceed ashore was getting their cabins locked. The key stewards were sometimes hard to find.'

Captain Mortleman-Lewis recalls his service in the *Strathaird* as the Staff Captain: 'The main duties of staff captains in those days were passenger entertainment and, to that end, they had to form a passengers' entertainment committee. It was not like today, where the entertainment staff are all highly professional. However, we managed to put on some very enjoyable events with various "theme" nights, and I also recall organizing a fun-fair on the Boat Deck with varied stalls found in such fairs manned by crew members, with the proceeds going to charity. One, now very notable, passenger on my first outward voyage was the then recently

77

The *Strathnaver* at Southampton in the 1950s. She is passing the Orient liner *Orcades* and the ill-fated troopship *Empire Windrush*.

(FotoFlite)

The *Stratheden* at Southampton.

married Rolf Harris returning to Australia for the opening of television in Perth. Throughout the voyage he delighted in entertaining the children in the afternoons and the adults after dinner in the evening, with his own particular brand of entertainment, something which he still does to this day. Needless to say he was a great asset to me on my "makee learn" voyage.'

On 14 January 1953 the *Strathmore* left Tilbury Landing Stage with more than 900 passengers and cargo on board for India and Australia, but as she reached Holehaven near Southend she developed machinery problems and was forced to return to Gravesend, where she was anchored overnight. As the trouble involved a bearing on her starboard propeller shaft and necessitated dry docking the ship, all the passengers, including Air Vice-Marshall Sir Robert George, who was on his way to take up his appointment as Governor of South Australia, were disembarked and the majority were accommodated in hotels at the company's expense. They eventually sailed on Wednesday 21 January, a week late, and the delay had meant a lot of hard work for both the dock staff and the ship's company.

In June 1953, with the impending entry into service of the 29,000-ton liners, *Arcadia* and *Iberia,* the P&O Company announced that it had decided to convert the first two *Straths,* the *Strathaird* and the *Strathnaver,* into one-class ships carrying tourist class passengers only. However, before this the *Strathnaver* took part in the Coronation Naval Review on 15 June 1953 to celebrate the coronation of Her Majesty Queen Elizabeth. Ships from the Royal Navy, Dominion and foreign navies, in addition to a number of merchant ships, assembled off Spithead, among them the *Strathnaver* which had been chartered by the government to take official guests to see the Review. The liner had arrived at Southampton from Australia with over 900 passengers on Saturday 13 June, and on the morning of Monday 15 June she was ready to receive her guests. The story is told by the *Strathnaver's* Master, Captain C.E. Pollit: 'Shortly before noon on Monday 15 June, *Strathnaver* left her berth at Southampton and followed the *Orcades* and *Pretoria Castle* down Southampton Water. On passing Calshot Light Vessel a magnificent sight came into view, away to the eastward, at anchor in the Solent, a vast concourse of ships, dressed overall, waiting for the moment when HM the Queen should pass by in the despatch vessel HMS *Surprise*[*] to review her fleet. Turning east and passing a line of merchant ships at anchor, the three liners altered course to pass between the line of aircraft-carriers and foreign men-of-war. Among the latter the Russian cruiser *Sverdlov* presented a particularly smart appearance. After

*Laid down in 1944 as the Loch-Class Frigate *Loch Carron,* but completed in March 1945 as the despatch vessel *Surprise*

Following the end of the war, the atmosphere of the pre-war days was almost re-created on the P&O liners in the 1950s. Here passengers play deck tennis on the *Strathaird's* Sports Deck.

(N. Pound)

(N. Pound)

Passengers enjoy a game of deck cricket on the *Strathaird's* Boat Deck.

The *Stratheden's* ill-fated motor lifeboat No 16 is lowered from the liner at the start of its mercy mission to rescue the crew of the Greek trawler *Iason*.

(Author's Collection)

passing these ships the three liners headed out to sea towards the Nab, in order to turn and take up their position in the procession astern of the *Surprise*. Shortly after 3pm the Trinity House yacht *Patricia* was seen clearing Portsmouth Harbour, followed a few minutes later by HMS *Surprise*, flying the Royal Standard at the main, the flag of the Lord High Admiral at the fore and the Union flag at the gaff. As these ships came into view there was a salute of 21 guns fired by the assembled fleet. At 3.30pm the *Patricia*, followed by the *Surprise*, turned into the line of ships and the Review had begun. It was a grand and unforgettable experience for those on board the three liners as they passed in procession through those lines of anchored ships, all dressed and manned and hearing the cheers of their ships' companies as they acclaimed Her Majesty. The Review over, *Strathnaver* and the other two liners anchored in positions at the end of the lines of men-of-war and not far from the Royal Yacht.' Another P&O employee, who was doing his national service as a seaman on HMS *Implacable*, David Ryall, describes the *Strathnaver* herself: 'Following *Surprise* was the *Redpole*, carrying other members of the Royal Family, the *Orcades, Pretoria Castle* and the *Strathnaver*, looking beautifully white and graceful as she sailed past. She seemed proud to be following Her Majesty on this great day, as I am sure were all those on board.' For Captain Pollit there was praise from the Admiralty, '...on the high-quality seamanship he displayed in navigating his ship at slow speed through narrow channels in difficult conditions of wind and tide.'

The first of the two *Straths* to be converted to 'one-class tourist' was the *Strathaird* and the work took place in March 1954. To accommodate the larger number of passengers, which would be 1,334 including 82 children in cots, the de luxe cabins were converted to six-berth rooms and 174 upper pullman berths were installed in other former first class cabins. In the forward dining saloon 42 extra seats were fitted, together with additional tables. The *Strathaird* made her first voyage in this new role on 8 April 1954. The *Strathnaver* underwent her conversion in July that year and Jim Buy recalls the last voyage as a two-class ship: 'It is always unfortunate to be aboard a ship when it is about to be structurally altered and be changed from a first class liner. Service during this last first class voyage consequently suffered. Once we were transferred to "one-class tourist" we carried a considerable number of £10 (assisted passage) emigrants and the cabins de luxe, being converted to six-berth cabins, were obviously suitable for a large migrant family. I remember that one large family of mother, father and ten children occupied two of these cabins. The Press wished to photograph them in Fremantle and the mother was quite surprised when she was asked whether they were Roman Catholics.'

In March 1955 the *Stratheden* was involved in a courageous rescue at sea which, sadly turned into a terrible tragedy. The liner, under the command of Captain Kenneth A.H. Cummins, was homeward bound from Australia, and having left Port Said on Friday 11 March 1955 was due to call at Marseilles four days later. At 11.20am (one hour ahead of GMT), on Sunday 13 March, the *Stratheden* was steaming north-west through the Ionian Sea in a Force 8 gale, considerable seas and a heavy swell, when the ship's radio

officer received a distress message from a Greek trawler, *Iason*, which was sinking in the stormy seas. Captain Cummins altered course and after three hours steaming he reached the Greek ship at 4.12pm that day. A few minutes later No 16 motor lifeboat, in the charge of Third Officer James M. Bower, was lowered. The story can be taken up by Mr Colin Suckling, the Assistant Engineer, who was one of the crew members of No 16 motor boat: 'Once our boat was in the water it was difficult to see the Greek ship. We could make out the smoke floats dropped by the aircraft and made towards them as best we could. Arriving at the *Iason* we found she had a starboard list down by the stern, and stern first onto the seas. Up to this time the lifeboat had shipped very little water.' Captain Alex Ctipatakos of the *Iason* explains his experiences: 'While I was exchanging cables, my sub-captain notified me that he could see a vessel on the horizon. In fact I noticed after a short while that the vessel was a passenger ship, proceeding towards us at full speed. I placed the entire crew on the upper deck. The lifeboat arrived near my ship and from it they called to us to throw ourselves into the sea and that they would pick us up.' The story is taken up again by Colin Suckling: 'Two men jumped into the water from the port side, but they were quickly swept away. The Third Officer manoeuvred the boat and they were picked up after about ten minutes. It was decided then to remain astern of the ship and let the men be swept down towards us. The seas were too heavy to allow us to keep the boat in any one position, so several runs were made along the ship and all the crew were taken off. We turned around and headed back towards the *Stratheden*.'

They had taken on board all the remaining 15 men from the *Iason*, and it appeared that the rescue was going to be successful, but as Colin Suckling explains, 'The seas had got considerably worse and the wind was taking the tops off the waves, making it difficult to see very far and on several occasions we lost sight of our own ship. We began to ship a little water and I asked the quartermaster aft to find a bucket and pass it up forward to try and reduce the level of water, leaving the Third Officer to concentrate on getting us back. We were trying to get leeward of the *Stratheden* but were unable to do so because of the heavy seas. We were a little astern and trying to make towards the *Stratheden* when the first of three heavy waves broke over the boat's bow. The Third Officer ordered everyone aft, but the other two waves rolled into the boat and she sank to engine-room level, overturned and sank stern first.'

On the *Stratheden's* bridge Captain Cummins saw the lifeboat, '...returning and she was heading, more or less, for the *Stratheden*. Whilst she was proceeding she seemed to be swerving a little off her course and was about 300 feet away from the ship on the port quarter abreast of the stern when she seemed to take a plunge and disappeared and I could no longer see her. I rushed across the bridge and saw a group of people in the water surrounding what was, I presumed, the submerged lifeboat.' Captain Cummins immediately gave orders for a second boat to be lowered but, although the engine of this boat had been running whilst in the falls, once it was in the water it stubbornly refused to start. Captain Cummins recalled this boat and steamed the *Stratheden* in a circle in order to bring the starboard side to the lee side and get to windward of the men in the water. As soon as he had completed this manoeuvre he ordered another two boats away and they managed to rescue seven survivors who were in the water.

The story is taken up once again by Colin Suckling, who was one of the seven to be rescued: 'Some of the buoyancy tanks came out as the boat overturned and were made very good use of. The Third Officer and Mr Ryan, one of the quartermasters, managed to get a tank and Donald Rigden (another quartermaster), and I another. Three Greeks and a few seamen joined our party, but very soon the seamen drifted away. Soon afterwards we were joined by another Greek and one seaman. This is how we remained until we were picked up.' In fact Mr Suckling had remained in contact with the Third Officer and Quartermaster Ryan for a time by shouting, but this soon became impossible due to the noise of the wind and sea.

Sadly 19 men were lost, eight of whom were from the *Stratheden's* boat, including James Bower the Third Officer, Quartermaster Joseph Ryan and six of the liner's Asian seamen. For the remaining hours of daylight and up to 11pm that night the *Stratheden's* boats continued to search the area and then Captain Cummins circled the area for the rest of the night until 9am the next morning. All the time the high winds, torrential rain and heavy seas hampered the lookouts and they were unable to use the searchlights. By mid-morning of 14 March it was clear that there were no further survivors and the *Stratheden* resumed her voyage to Marseilles. She arrived there at 6.30am on 16 March and sailed again at 4pm the same day. Her short stop off Brixham in Devon was cancelled and she proceeded to Tilbury Landing Stage to disembark her passengers. A report on the tragic incident found that, '...great credit was due to Captain Cummins, his officers and men who took part in the rescue operations for their courage and persistence, and deep regret is expressed at the loss of life involved.' Three months later, when the *Strathnaver* was steaming through the Mediterranean and was approaching Port Said, a passing Greek tanker, *Atlantic Lady*, signalled, 'Thanks from a Greek seaman saved by the *Stratheden.*' This gave a lot of pleasure and pride to the whole P&O fleet.

At this time there were other, happier memories, and Mr Eric Birchall, a laundryman, who made a number of voyages in the *Strathmore* during 1955 and 1956 recalls one of his colleagues: 'I have vivid memories of Trevor Stanford, a tourist class baggage steward who was a wonderful pianist. He had permission from the Chief Steward to use the piano in the tourist class children's playroom. During voyages I made in the *Strathmore* I enjoyed sitting with Trevor, with a drink and listening to his wonderful playing. Some years later I was watching a music show on television and there was Trevor playing "Side Saddle", the tune which went to the top of the hit parade - yes it was Russ Conway.'

In the mid-1950s the European colonial powers had serious problems in both the Middle and Far East and, with a great deal of their trade carried out in these regions of the world, it was inevitable that the ships of the P&O would be involved in these colonial disputes. In July 1954 it had been agreed that British troops would be withdrawn progressively from the base in the Canal Zone by the middle of 1956, for it

was clear that Egypt would not agree to a renewal of the Anglo-Egyptian Treaty when it became due in 1957. Troopships were busy bringing home and redeploying the 80,000 British troops (the equivalent of over two divisions), and the P&O were able to help out with this task. In January 1956, despite being delayed by nine days because of boiler trouble, the *Strathaird* embarked the advance parties of the 1st Battalions of the Welsh and Irish Guards at Port Said, the last infantry units of the British Army in the Canal Zone. In June that year, by which time the last British troops had left the Canal Zone, the *Strathnaver* was in Port Said and it was ironic that, at the request of the Egyptian government, she was dressed overall. In addition however, as there was no sign of the Union Flag ashore, the Chief Officer decided to hoist a 12-yard Red Ensign on the stern which in the Second Officer's words, '...assumed a mighty magnificence all its own, as it floated lazily and gracefully on a gentle breeze.'

However, in July 1956, less than a month after the last British troops had left Egypt, President Nasser nationalized the Suez Canal and this led, three months later, to the ill-fated Anglo-French invasion of Port Said and the Canal. In the weeks running up to the invasion the political negotiations dragged on and the tensions mounted. In mid-September that year, P&O announced that most of its ships would divert from their usual routes via Suez and sail instead via Cape Town. The *Strathmore* was homeward bound in the Indian Ocean at the time and, after making her calls at Colombo and Bombay, she then steamed south-south-west for Durban, Cape Town and Las Palmas, arriving in London on 10 October. She had been due to leave for Australia five days later, but this sailing was cancelled and instead she was ordered to make a special sailing on 26 October 1956, via Suez, to Bombay, where she was due to arrive 16 days later, on 11 November. In view of the fact that calls by the company's ships to Aden, Bombay and Colombo were being cancelled, it was considered necessary to make this special voyage.

Meanwhile voyages for the other three *Straths* were being revised. The *Strathnaver,* which left London on 18 September 1956, steamed to Sydney via Cape Town, and the *Stratheden,* which left Sydney on 26 September, returned to London by way of the Cape. Towards the end of October 1956, with the nationalization of the Canal having been accomplished, and with shipping running remarkably smoothly, although Anglo-French forces were continuing to build up in the Eastern Mediterranean, it seemed to most observers that the seemingly interminable political negotiations would eventually reach an amicable solution. In view of this there did not seem to be any reason to alter the *Strathmore's* special sailing to Bombay, and she left Tilbury on 26 October 1956, as scheduled. She arrived in Malta five days later on the eve of the Anglo-French invasion of Egypt, to find Grand Harbour buzzing with military activity as the troop transports and supply ships which would follow up the initial assaults, left for Port Said. She was ordered to remain at Malta until the military situation became clearer and two days later, on 2 November, with the invasion in full swing and the Suez Canal well and truly blocked, she was ordered to steam west and resume her voyage to India by way of Gibraltar, Las Palmas, Cape Town and Durban, and she arrived in Bombay on 29

November, 18 days behind schedule. It was the end of December 1956 before the *Strathmore* returned to London. Meanwhile, at the other end of the Suez Canal, the *Strathaird*, which was homeward bound, was ordered to remain at Aden until the situation became clearer, but as the invasion got under way she too was re-routed round the Cape, and for the next six months until the summer of 1957, all four vessels used the long route via Cape Town and the Southern Ocean. Surprisingly, when they did start to use the Suez Canal again, the people of Port Said and Suez showed no animosity towards passengers or crew members and it was 'business as usual' once more.

In December 1957 the *Strathaird* left Tilbury for Sydney, where she arrived in mid-January 1958. From Sydney she made a ten-day cruise to Wellington and Auckland in New Zealand. It was the vessel's first visit to the two ports since her trooping days during the Second World War. She disembarked her passengers back in Sydney on 28 January 1958, and sailed three days later for home. On this voyage she became involved in a hangover from the Dutch colonial problems in Indonesia. Unlike the British officials and businessmen, who mainly considered their colonial possessions as 'staging posts' in their careers, many Dutch nationals thought of what used to be the Netherlands East Indies as 'home'. Therefore, in late 1957, when President Achmed Sukarno of Indonesia ordered all Dutch nationals out of his country, there were thousands of these refugees who required transport from Djakarta (formerly Batavia) to Rotterdam. Several P&O liners were chartered by the Netherlands government to assist with the task and of course the 'one-class tourist' ships were ideal. On her outward voyage the *Strathaird* had carried nearly 500 assisted passage emigrants from London to Sydney, but on her return voyage she had, as usual, large numbers of empty berths. She called at Djakarta on 15 February 1958 and the story is best told by one of her crew members, Mr Arthur Smith of Paignton: 'After leaving Fremantle the ship was diverted to Djakarta in Indonesia, arriving on 15 February, in order to repatriate Dutch nationals. Surly armed guards were placed on the gangways and very few people were allowed ashore. I personally, as baggage steward, had to go on shore to check which baggage had to come on board. After doing this in the godown on the jetty I went to go back up the gangway, whereupon a guard pushed the muzzle of his rifle in my stomach and wouldn't let me back on board. After much explaining he finally let me go. Although the *Strathaird* was a one-class ship, all the passengers from Australia who were berthed aft were transferred to the forward accommodation and the Dutch were berthed aft. They were a very happy crowd although they didn't appear to have much money, presumably the armed guards took it from them before they embarked. I mention this fact because they were giving original water-colours away to certain crew members, in lieu of gratuities. They did not seem to be unhappy to be leaving Indonesia under President Sukarno.'

On this homeward voyage the *Strathaird* called at Marseilles and on 9 March 1958 reached Rotterdam, where she remained for four days before sailing for Tilbury, arriving on 14 March.

As the 1950s drew to a close and with work on the big new passenger ship *Canberra* well under way, it was clear that the careers of the first two 'White Sisters', *Strathnaver* and *Strathaird*, were coming to an end.

The *Strathaird* arrives at Tilbury for the last time on Saturday 17 June 1961. She had left Australia the previous month and passed the brand new *Canberra* in the Mediterranean, just out from Port Said.

(P&O)

Chapter Fourteen

The Final Years

In 1960 the *Strathmore* was chartered by a new travel company, Global Tours, for round voyages between Sydney and Marseilles, picking up passengers at Naples as well for the return journey. The vessel operated one-class for these round trips and Captain Mortleman-Lewis believes that it was the happy atmosphere which prevailed during the voyages which helped to put Global 'on the map'. All four ships continued to make cruises and in April 1961 the *Stratheden* called at St Vincent in the Cape Verde Islands during an Atlantic Islands cruise. In May and June that year the *Strathnaver* cruised from Sydney to the Pacific Ocean ports of Pago Pago, Suva, Noumea and, for the first time, Haymen Island. Despite being a rather 'elderly' ship she was still very popular, carrying in the region of 1,000 passengers on each trip. In October 1961 she reverted to two-class operation for her homeward voyage from Brisbane to London. The forward section was reserved for passengers embarking in Australia and the after section for the passengers embarking in Bombay. By this time the mass immigration of Asians into Britain was at its height and these passengers, with their different culture and lifestyle, were a trial for the crews of the P&O liners. The stewards in particular had their work cut out trying to stop them cooking their curries and chapattis on primus stoves in their cabins.

On 24 March 1961, with the revolutionary new *Canberra* only two months away from completion, P&O made the following press release: 'P&O-Orient Lines announce that the 22,500-ton passenger liner *Strathaird* is to be withdrawn from service when she arrives in London on 18 June 1961.' Passengers who were already booked for voyages after that date were offered alternative accommodation. The old ship was given her final farewells from the Australian ports in May that year. On 8 May 1961, at Sydney, there was a luncheon held on board for 150 old friends and she finally left the port at 7pm the next day. On 19 May she made her final call at Fremantle and the ship was a splendid sight, dressed overall with a 177 ft paying off pennant flying. On 8 June 1961, when the *Strathaird* was six hours out of Port Said and westbound, she passed the *Canberra* which was eastbound on her maiden voyage. The older ship, flying her paying off pennant, steamed quickly past *Canberra*, and both ships' whistles blew in greeting. Captain A.E. Clay, commanding the *Strathaird*, signalled to Commodore Wild of the *Canberra*: 'You look magnificent and all in *Strathaird* wish you a happy and successful voyage and from the old to the new, *Strathaird* bids you farewell.' Commodore Wild replied: 'You too look magnificent with your paying off pennant flying gaily. You look a gracious and not too elderly lady. All well here.'

On the morning of 24 June 1961, the *Strathaird* left Tilbury in ballast, bound for the breaker's yard in Hong Kong.

(Alex Duncan)

A view of the *Strathaird* shortly after she arrived in Hong Kong for demolition. She is looking rather weather-beaten and worn and it was not long before the steel from her hull was used to build the high-rise flats of Hong Kong.

(Hong Kong Government Information Service)

The *Strathnaver* at Tilbury towards the end of her career. *(Alex Duncan)*

The *Strathnaver* moored off Ngautaukok, near to Hong Kong's Kai Tak Airport. This photograph would have been before February 1963, when the author saw her alongside and being stripped of her internal fittings. *(P&O)*

The *Strathmore* at Tilbury towards the end of her career with the P&O Company. *(E.H. Cole)*

The *Stratheden* on the Thames. *(Alex Duncan)*

The *Stratheden*, outward bound from London, passes Canvey Island on 15 May 1963. *(FotoFlite)*

The *Stratheden* anchored off Gravesend in the final stages of her career with P&O. *(E.H. Cole)*

A stern view of the *Marianna Latsis*, ex-*Strathmore* (left) and the *Henrietta Latsis*, ex-*Stratheden* (right), in dock at Piraeus.

(*G.L. Jones*)

The *Strathaird* had been sold to the Shun Fung Ironworks of Hong Kong for £382,500 and it was a condition of the sale that, '...demolition must begin two months after delivery and must be completed a year later.' She arrived in Tilbury early on Saturday 17 June 1961 and exactly one week later, at 7.30am on 24 June, she left the port, this time in ballast and commanded by Captain D.F. West. Just four weeks later, on 24 July, she arrived in Hong Kong where at 10am on 27 July, Mr L.Y. Leung, the Managing Director of Shun Fung Ironworks, signed the formal delivery documents and took possession of the *Strathaird*, the largest ship to be scrapped in Hong Kong. The P&O house-flag was lowered from the ship's mast-head for the last time and Captain West, with his 84-man crew left the ship. Captain West had served six years in the *Strathaird* in every capacity from Junior Second Officer to Master. He had also met his future wife on the ship whilst serving as Second Officer in 1947. Perhaps his most interesting voyage was the delivery trip to the scrapyard and as he commented at the time, 'It felt somehow strange walking on board so quiet and empty a ship, which was once so full of life.'

By the spring of 1962 the old ship had virtually disappeared but she had in fact contributed to the Hong Kong skyline. Her steel, after it had been melted down and re-rolled into reinforcing bars, was used in the construction of new 'skyscraper' blocks and even the new terminal buildings at Kai Tak Airport contained much of the liner's steel in their structure.

The *Strathnaver* was the next of the *Straths* to go to the scrapyard. Only five months after the *Strathaird* was handed over in Hong Kong, P&O announced on 12 December 1961 that *Strathnaver*, now outward bound to Sydney, was to be withdrawn on completion of the voyage which she had started only five days earlier. Originally it had been planned to keep her in service until late 1962, but there had been a sudden drop in the number of emigrants from Britain to Australia, which caused the Australian government to cancel large numbers of provisional bookings for assisted passage berths which had been scheduled for the first five months of 1962. The *Strathnaver* was due back into Tilbury on 23 February 1962 and passengers with bookings after this date were offered alternative berths in other company ships, including the *Canberra*. Once again the ship was given a suitable farewell from the Australian ports and only eight days before she arrived back in Tilbury, P&O announced that, like her sister, the *Strathnaver* had been sold to the Shun Fung Ironworks of Hong Kong, in this case for £325,000.

The *Strathnaver* arrived off Gravesend at 6am on Friday 23 February 1962 and half an hour later she was secured alongside Tilbury Landing Stage, where passengers disembarked for the last time. Later that day she went alongside 33 berth in Tilbury Docks where destoring took place. Six days later, at 5pm on Thursday 1 March she left the Thames for the delivery voyage. She was in ballast and had on board a 77-man crew commanded by Captain W.N. Eade, who had served in the *Strathnaver* on and off since her maiden voyage. After making her final transit of the Suez Canal on 11 March and calling at Aden and Singapore, the old ship arrived in Hong Kong on 1 April and the following day the sale contract was signed by both Captain Eade and Mr L.Y. Leung. It was said that the process of dismantling

the ship would begin almost immediately, but this was not the case for when I visited Hong Kong for three weeks in late February 1963, the rather derelict *Strathnaver* was berthed alongside the breaker's yard at Ngautaukok near Kai Tak Airport. The vessel had a heavy list to port and her lifeboats were gone. Her once gleaming white hull was brown with rust, as was her buff funnel, but breaking up had not started in earnest. However, when I returned to the colony seven months later she had gone.

With the demise of the *Strathaird* and the imminent withdrawal of the *Strathnaver*, the last two 'White Sisters' were converted for 'one-class tourist' operation. The work took place in late 1961 when both ships were given berths for 1,200 passengers, most of whom would be travelling under the Australian government's assisted passage scheme. The *Stratheden's* first sailing from Tilbury after conversion was on 7 November 1961 with a minimum fare for independent passengers of £160 for a berth in a cabin for five or six. The conversion work on the *Strathmore* took place in December 1961 and she made her first one-class voyage from Tilbury to Far Eastern ports and Brisbane on 6 January 1962, sailing via Suez, Singapore, Hong Kong, Yokohama and Manila.

Mrs Patricia Hanks of Windsor recalls her service as a Female Assistant Purser in the *Stratheden* in mid-1962, after she had spent a year in the *Orcades*: 'My long-awaited posting came and to my chagrin I learnt I was to sail in one of the company's "old faithfuls". It was with mixed feelings, therefore, that I made my way down to Tilbury, not quite knowing what to expect. As the ships in port came closer I could guess which one was to be my home for the next three months. She was easily distinguishable because of her superstructure and the fact that she had rather an elongated funnel, which looked very outdated. Immediately I boarded her I sensed a different atmosphere, this was a ship used now almost solely for the carriage of emigrants from the UK to Australia and, as such, many internal alterations had taken place. I soon found out that we were also carrying immigrants homewards, picking up some 1,000 Indian passengers from Bombay, another story altogether, destined mainly for the UK. It was, therefore, with some consternation as to what lay ahead and the work involved, that I and my colleagues set sail from Tilbury that bright June afternoon (12 June 1962). One advantage of starting out with a completely full complement of passengers was the fact that we did not embark any more *en route* to Australia, which made our work somewhat easier, but with such large numbers of passengers it was almost as bad. To add to the general confusion we had over 500 children under the age of 12 on board. The combined noise was something to be heard to be believed and it was almost impossible to walk down the alleyways without tripping over small infants rolling round the deck. The main difficulty was organizing such large numbers, sittings at mealtimes, cinema shows, deck sports and entertainments. The organization of the 500 children was a problem, but this was helped considerably by the fact that we took on two supernumerary staff to assist and converted one of the after lounges into a nursery.

The ship was entirely without air-conditioning and the sole method of ventilation was by means of punkah louvres which, in the Red Sea, just circulated the hot air and on occasions the temperature in the cabins was over 100°F. However, many people from G and H Decks were given the opportunity of sleeping up on the open deck on camp beds. A lot of people took advantage of this and the scene was rather reminiscent of a wartime troopship. It certainly made one's nightly strolls on deck rather hazardous. Every way one turned there was a camp bed, whose occupant was either fast asleep or gazing at the tropical sky.

Many of our passengers under the government scheme did not know their final destination in Australia, or indeed at which port they were to disembark. Neither did we for that matter, and it made life difficult in the purser's office - we were apt to find our numbers substantially depleted when more people were told to disembark at a certain port, or vice versa. Our passengers were a very philosophical crowd on the whole and, with few exceptions, were wonderful people to deal with. It was interesting to hear about their hopes and aspirations for their new lives on the other side of the world from the "home" they had known. However, it was a welcome relief, therefore, to arrive in Sydney and have a deserted ship for six whole days. It was quite eerie after the noise and hubbub we had grown accustomed to.'

The two ships continued with their migrant voyages to Australia during 1962 and they undertook cruises from both the UK and Sydney. However, on 13 November 1962, P&O announced that both vessels were to be withdrawn from service during the following 18 months. It was also said that their future employment was under discussion, but it was clear that their careers with P&O were drawing to a close. The first to go was the *Strathmore* and she left Tilbury for her final Australian voyage on 20 June 1963. In July and August that year she was feted in all the Australian ports before setting out for London once again, where she arrived on 4 September. On 23 October 1963, whilst the *Strathmore* was on a Mediterranean cruise and the *Stratheden* was one day out of Tilbury from Sydney, it was announced that P&O had sold both vessels to a Greek shipowner, Mr John S. Latsis, of Athens. Mr Latsis proposed to use them for most of the year as hotel ships in the Mediterranean, and during other periods they were to be used for Mr Latsis' pilgrim service. The *Strathmore* completed her final cruise at Tilbury on October 27 1963 and during her four-day stop in the port various items were removed from the ship and, at the request of Lt-Colonel Sir Martin Gilliat, the Queen Mother's Private Secretary, the tapestry of Glamis Castle, the portrait of the Duchess of York and a photograph of the ship's launching ceremony were sent to Her Majesty. Perhaps the letter from Sir Donald Anderson to Lt-Colonel Gilliat summed up the old ship: 'Of all the pre-war passenger ships which survived the war *Strathmore* has always had a very special place in the minds of P&O sea staff. She was always considered by far the best of the five *Straths* and was always the happiest.'

The *Strathmore* left Southampton on the last day of October 1963 and a week later, on 7 November, she was handed over to her new owners in Piraeus. She was renamed *Marianna Latsis* and after a short refit she was soon engaged in ferrying pilgrims to Jedda, from where they travelled on to Mecca.

The *Stratheden's* final line voyage to Australia for P&O terminated at Tilbury on 24 October 1963 and after being laid up at Portland between 9 and 27 November, she was chartered by the Travel Savings Association during December 1963 and January 1964. They had planned two nine-day cruises to Casablanca, Gibraltar and Lisbon, the first of which started on 1 December 1963. These were followed by a 15-day cruise to Madeira and the Canaries, which started on 20 December and a 33-day cruise to the West Indies, leaving Southampton on 4 January 1964. The prices of the cruises started at £2 a day, cheaper even, allowing for inflation, than the 'pound a day' cruises of the early 1930s. The charter was due to finish upon the vessel's arrival in Southampton on 5 February 1964, and for its duration P&O would provide the ship's company and normal 'one-class tourist' services. All the booking arrangements, shore excursions and entertainment was to be provided by the charterers.

It was whilst the *Stratheden* was on her third voyage to Madeira and the Canaries that she became involved in the tragedy of the Greek ship MV *Lakonia*. The *Lakonia* (19,040grt), had been built in 1930 as the Nederland Royal Mail ship *Johan van Oldenbarnevelt* for the Rotterdam - Batavia route. She had been withdrawn from service in February 1963 and sold to the Greek General Steam Navigation Company, as an addition to their fleet. Renamed *Lakonia*, she had been refitted in Genoa and had sailed from Southampton on Thursday 19 December 1963, her first port of call being Madeira, where she was due four days later on the morning of Monday 23 December. She was actually 180 miles north of Madeira and 250 miles west of Casablanca, in a position 35°-00'N/15°-15'W on the afternoon of Sunday 22 December, when fire broke out in a hairdressing salon. The conflagration quickly took hold and with great confusion amongst both the crew and passengers, the incident soon became a disaster. A number of ships, together with aircraft from the USAF base in the Azores rushed to the scene, and at 7pm that evening the *Stratheden*, which had sailed on her cruise from Southampton the day after the *Lakonia*, arrived. The rescue of survivors was being co-ordinated by the freighter *Montcalm* and the *Stratheden* was able to embark the four most badly injured survivors in order that they could receive better medical attention in the ship's hospital. She also provided 240 loaves of bread to supplement the *Montcalm's* rations and a large quantity of clothing which had been donated by the *Stratheden's* passengers. The *Stratheden* left the scene soon after taking on the injured and set course for Madeira, which was her scheduled port of call, in order to land them for hospital treatment. Unfortunately, the most badly burned of the four died during the voyage, before the *Stratheden* reached Funchal at 6am on 24 December 1963, the first of the rescue ships to arrive at Madeira.

On 10 February 1964, five days after her charter was completed, the *Stratheden* followed her sister to the Greek port of Piraeus, where she arrived seven days later. She too had been sold to John S. Latsis for the pilgrim trade, and she was renamed *Henrietta Latsis*. For the next five years the two ships became a familiar sight in Piraeus, the Eastern Mediterranean and the Red Sea. In 1966 they exchanged names and three years later, in May 1969, they were sold to Italian shipbreakers for just over £1 million. So ended the careers of the last of P&O's 'White Sisters' of the 1930s.

PRINCIPAL PARTICULARS:

	Strathnaver/Strathaird	Strathmore	Stratheden/Strathallan
Length Overall:	664ft	665ft	664$\frac{1}{2}$ft
Length B.P:	630ft	630ft	630ft
Breadth Moulded:	80ft	82ft	82ft
Gross Tonnage:	22,547/22,281	23,482	23,722/23,722
Net Tonnage:	13,620/13,242	14,144	14,127/14,127
Propulsion Machinery:	Twin propellers driven by electric motors, powered by two turbo-alternators. 28,000 SHP. 22knots.	Twin propellers driven by Parsons single-reduction steam turbines 24,000 SHP. 21 knots.	Twin propellers driven by Parsons single-reduction steam turbines 24,000 SHP. 21 knots.
Passengers:			
First Class:	498	445	448
Tourist Class:	670	665	563
Crew:	487	509	563

Acknowledgements

Special thanks to Mr Don Smith and Mr Duncan Smedley for the loan of their superb colour transparancies. Readers wishing to purchase duplicates of Mr Smith's slides should write to 7 Chapel Court, Hambleton, Selby, Yorkshire, YO8 9YF.

Thanks also to Mr Ian Spashett of FotoFlite for permission to use his company's magnificent photographs. Readers wishing to purchase prints from FotoFlite should contact FotoFlite, Littlestone Road, New Romney, Kent, TN28 8NP.

R. & J. Allan, Glasgow: E. Birchell, Essex: Captain M.V.N. Bradford CBE RD, Worcestershire: J.H. Buy, Hampshire: J.K. Byass, Yorkshire: M. Cassar, Malta: J.A. Clifford, Middlesex: E.H. Cole, Middlesex: P. Cross, Kent: A. Davies, VSEL, Barrow-in-Furness: D. Deere, Marine Publications International Ltd: A. Duncan, Kent: S.F. Edney, London: W.G. Elton, Suffolk: M. Esterkin, P&O: Mrs O. Evans, Suffolk: Captain R.N. Firth, Hampshire: A. Forsyth, Southampton City Museum: Captain I. Gibb, P&O: P. Gourley, Kent: Mrs P.A. Hanks, Berkshire: G. Harding, Wiltshire: A. Hernandez, Miami, USA: J.N. Hulse, Sussex: F.F. Irons, Essex: G.L. Jones, Hampshire: P. Kemp, IWM, London: Mr C. Lowe, New Milton, Hampshire: P. Miles, Worcestershire: H.W Mills, Hampshire: The late Mr G. Milne, Aberdeen: Captain E. Mortleman-Lewis, Hampshire: F.A. O'Conner, Essex: B.A. Ohlson, Dorset: Mrs Lyn Palmer, P&O: A.E. Piper, London: N. Pound, P&O: S. Rabson, P&O: E.J. Read, Hampshire: W. Richardson, Spain: J. D. Sankey, Ulverstone, Cumbria: The late Mr L. Sanderson, West Ewell, Surrey: G.C. Shaw OBE, Essex: J. Simpson, P&O: D. Smedley, Hertfordshire: A. Smith, Devon: F.J. Smith, Suffolk: G.S.S. Stone, Leicestershire: R.C. Temple, Hampshire: Captain C.B. Thompson RD, New Zealand: R.G. Todd, National Maritime Museum, Greenwich, London: A. Vicary, Suffolk: Commodore J.F. Wacher CBE RD, Hampshire: A.B. Webzell, P&O: Mrs A. Weston, NSW, Australia: B. Wexham, Vickers PLC, London: F. Witcombe, Sussex: L. Wyeth, Lincolnshire: Finally thanks to my wife Freda and my daughters Caroline & Louise.

Other Titles From FAN PUBLICATIONS:

P&O's *Canberra & Sea Princess* £6.95

Famous British Liners Series:
Vol 1 *SS Oriana* - The Last Great Orient Liner £6.95
Vol 2 *SS Viceroy of India* - P&O's First Electric Cruise Liner £6.95
Vol 3 *Arcadia & Iberia* - P&O's Sisters For The 1950s £6.95
Vol 4 *SS Aquitania* - Cunard's Atlantic Lady £7.95

UK & European readers add £1.50 p&p: Other overseas readers add £3.50 towards air mail postage.

Write now for further details to:
FAN PUBLICATIONS
17 Wymans Lane
Cheltenham
Glos GL51 9QA
England
Fax & Tel: 01242 580290